What's yellow and goes *click-click*?
A ball point banana

• • •

I'm collecting for the old folks' home.
Do you have anything to contribute?
Hang on and I'll fetch Granddad

• • •

What did one flea say to the other
flea?
"Shall we walk or take a cat?"

• • •

Why did the peanut complain to the
police?
'Cause he'd been assaulted.

• • •

Preserve wildlife—pickle a squirrel.

Published by Ballantine Books:

OH NO! NOT ANOTHER 1,000 JOKES FOR KIDS

1,000 JOKES FOR KIDS OF ALL AGES

1,000 KNOCK KNOCK JOKES FOR KIDS

1,000 MORE JOKES FOR KIDS

1,000 WHAT'S WHAT JOKES FOR KIDS

OH NO!
NOT ANOTHER
1,000 JOKES
FOR KIDS

by Michael Kilgarriff

BALLANTINE BOOKS • NEW YORK

ISBN 0-345-34035-3

This edition published by arrangement with Ward Lock Ltd.

Manufactured in the United States of America

First Ballantine Books Edition: June 1987
Third Printing: December 1987

Contents

The Bookworm's Banquet

or Literary Lunacies

My Golden Wedding	*by* Annie Versary
The Insurmountable Problem	*by* Major Setback
Crime Does Not Pay	*by* Laura Norder
A Load of Old Rubbish	*by* Stefan Nonsense
Tape Recording Made Easy	*by* Cass Ette
Don't Go Without Me	*by* Isa Cummin
Making the Most of Life	*by* Maxie Mumm
Making the Least of Life	*by* Minnie Mumm
When Shall We Meet Again?	*by* Miles Apart
The Arctic Ocean	*by* I.C. Waters
Scalp Disorders	*by* Dan Druff
Willie Win	*by* Betty Wont
Return of the Prodigal	*by* Greta Sonne
A Call for Assistance	*by* Linda Hand
Pain and Sorrow	*by* Ann Guish

Garden Design	*by* Lily Pond
Crossing the Road	*by* Luke Bothways
Sunday Service	*by* Neil Downe
The Laser Weapon	*by* Ray Gunn
Fade Away	*by* Peter Out
Into Battle	*by* Sally Forth
Diaper Making	*by* D. Sposable
Sweet Remembrance	*by* Valentine Card
The Japanese Way of Death	*by* Harri Kiri
Repairing Old Clothes	*by* Fred Bare
The Lady Artist	*by* Andrew Pictures
The Leaky Tap	*by* Constant Dripping
Summertime	*by* Clement Weather
The Lighthouse	*by* Eddy Stone
Don't Wake the Baby!	*by* Elsie Cries
The Worst Journey in the World	*by* Helen Back
Out for Six	*by* Esau Stars
The Strongman	*by* Everard Muscles
My Happiest Day	*by* Trudy Light
Karate for Beginners	*by* Flora Mugger
Are You a Millionaire?	*by* Jonah Lott
Pig Breeding	*by* Lena Bacon
Who Killed Cock Robin?	*by* U. Dunnit
Kidnapped	*by* Caesar Quick
The Haunted Room	*by* Hugo First
Forward the Bad	*by* Mr. Goal
Making Weatherproof Clothes	*by* Rainier Day
Late Again	*by* Misty Buss

2

Magic for Beginners	*by* Beatrix Ster
English Folk Customs	*by* Morris Dancer
Making Snack Meals	*by* San Widge
Discipline in the Home	*by* Wilma Child Begood

Cross-Purposes

What do you get if you cross...

—*a skunk and an owl?*
A bird that smells but doesn't give a hoot!

—*a cow and a camel?*
Lumpy milkshakes!

—*a sheepdog and a bunch of daisies?*
Collie-flowers!

4

—*a parrot and an alligator?*
Something that bites your head off and says "Polly want a cracker?!"

—*a parrot and an elephant?*
Something that tells everything it remembers.

—*an elephant and peanut butter?*
Either peanut butter that never forgets or an elephant that sticks to the roof of your mouth.

—*a kangaroo and a mink?*
A fur coat with pockets.

—*a sheep and a rainstorm?*
A wet blanket.

—*a pig and a zebra?*
Striped sausages.

—*a centipede and a parrot?*
  A walkie talkie.

—*a cow and a duck?*
  Queam Quackers.

Differences of Opinion

What's the difference between...

—*the Prince of Wales and a tennis ball?*
One is heir to the throne and the other is thrown into the air.

—*seasickness and an auction?*
One is the effects of a sail and the other is the sale of effects.

—*a cat and a comma?*
A cat has claws at the end of its paws and a comma has a pause at the end of its clause.

7

—*an orchestral conductor and an oven?*
One makes the beat and the other bakes the meat.

—*a flea-bitten dog and a bored guest?*
One is going to itch and the other is itching to go.

—*a good darts player and a violin case?*
One finds the middle and the other minds the fiddle.

—*an oak tree and a tight shoe?*
One makes acorns and the other makes corns ache.

—*a young lady and a fresh loaf?*
One is a well-bred maid and the other is a well-made bread.

—*a coyote and a flea?*
One howls on the prairie and the other prowls on the hairy.

—*a hungry man and a greedy man?*
One longs to eat and the other eats too long.

—*a rain gutter and a bad fielder?*
One catches drops and the other drops catches.

—*a stubborn donkey and a postage stamp?*
One you lick with a stick and the other you stick with a lick.

—*a farmer and a dressmaker?*
One gathers what he sows and the other sews what she gathers.

—*an iceberg and a clothes brush?*
One crushes boats and the other brushes coats.

—*a kangaroo and a lumberjack?*
One hops and chews and the other chops and hews.

—a soccer player and a well-behaved student?
One times passes well and the other passes the time well.

—sixteen ounces of butter and a loud piano player?
One weighs a pound and the other pounds away.

—an elephant and a cookie?
You can't dunk an elephant in your coffee.

—an old car and a classroom?
Not a lot—they both have a lot of nuts and a crank in the front!

—a thief and a church bell?
One steals from the people and the other peals from the steeple.

—a girl and a postage stamp?
One is a female and the other is a mail fee.

—a sick cow and an angry crowd?
   One moos badly and the other boos madly.

—a hill and a pill?
   One goes up and the other goes down.

Elephantasia

Why are elephants bad dancers?
'Cause they have two left feet.

What do you do if an elephant sneezes?
Get out of the way!

What happened to Ray when he was stepped on by an elephant?
He became an X-Ray.

When do elephants paint their toenails red?
When they want to hide in strawberry jam.

What did the grape say when an elephant stepped on it?
Not much—it just gave a little w(h)ine.

What's the best way to raise an elephant?
Use a crane.

How do you get an elephant into a telephone booth?
Open the door.

Is it difficult to bury a dead elephant?
Yes, it's a huge undertaking.

What would you do if an elephant sat in front of you at the movies?
Miss most of the film.

Why do elephants have flat feet?
From jumping out of tall trees.

Is the squirt from an elephant's trunk very powerful?
Of course—a jumbo jet can keep five hundred people in the air for hours at a time.

How do you make an elephant sandwich?
>First of all you get a *very* large loaf of bread . . .

What did the elephant say when the crocodile bit off his trunk?
>"I thuppothe you think thad's fuddy. . . ."

What's big and red and hides its face in the corner?
>An embarrassed elephant.

Why did the elephant cross the road?
>To pick up the squashed chicken.

Why do elephants wear sandals?
>To keep their feet from sinking in the sand.

Why do ostriches bury their heads in the sand?
>To see all the elephants who aren't wearing their sandals.

How do you get an elephant into a matchbox?
>Take out the matches first.

Why did the elephant take two trunks on his vacation?
    One to drink through and the other to swim in.

What do you do with a blue elephant?
    Cheer him up.

*If you shoot a white elephant with a white gun, what do you
    shoot a pink elephant with?*
    No, not a pink gun—you paint the elephant white
    then shoot it with a white gun . . .

What's grey and wrinkled and lights up?
    An electric elephant.

What do elephants do in the back of a Volkswagen?
    Play squash.

 What are the largest ants in the world?
    Eleph-ants.

15

Sick Humor

or Fits of Laughter

DOCTOR: "How is your husband's lumbago?"
WIFE: "Not too good. I rubbed his back with whiskey like you told me to and he broke his neck trying to lick it off!"

"Doctor! Doctor! Everyone keeps throwing me in the garbage!"

"Don't talk rubbish."

"Doctor! Doctor! I'm boiling up!"

"Just simmer down."

"Doctor! Doctor! Will this ointment clear up my zits?"

"I never make rash promises."

DOCTOR: "I'm sorry, Mr. Hassleblatt, but I've got bad news. However, I've also got good news. Which would you rather hear first?"

PATIENT: "Tell me the bad news first, doctor."

DOCTOR: "The bad news is that we've got to take off both your legs. The good news is that the man in the next bed wants to buy your slippers."

DOCTOR: "And how are you today, Mrs. Trample?"

PATIENT: "Well, doctor, you know you told me to have a glass of orange juice every night after a hot bath?"

DOCTOR: "Yes?"

PATIENT: "I managed to drink the orange juice all right but I've had an awful time trying to get the hot bath down."

"My doctor told me to take two of these pills on an empty stomach."

"Did they do any good?"

"I don't know. They keep rolling off in the night."

"Doctor! Doctor! I feel like a needle!"
"Yes, I see your point."

"Doctor, I think I've got the flu."
"Very well. Just put your tongue out and then stick your head out of the window."
"Will that make me better?"
"No, but I can't stand the woman who lives across the street . . ."

"Doctor! Doctor! My sister thinks she's an elevator."
"Tell her to come in."
"I can't. She doesn't stop at this floor."

A man went to the dentist, sat in the chair and immediately began shouting and screaming. "What's all the fuss about?" demanded the dentist. "I haven't touched your tooth yet."
"I know," said the patient, "but you're—aagh!—standing on my foot!"

"Doctor! Doctor! I feel I'm a goat!"
"Stop acting like a little kid."

"Doctor! Doctor! I just swallowed four red pool balls, three blue pool balls and two black pool balls!"

"Eat some greens and you'll be all right soon."

"Doctor! Doctor! I just swallowed a roll of film!"

"Let's hope nothing develops."

"Doctor! Doctor! Can you help me out?"

"Certainly. Which way did you come in?"

"I'm sorry to bother you, doctor, but it's my Dad. He keeps saying he wants to die."

"You did the right thing in sending for me."

"Tell me straight, doctor, is it serious?"

"Well, I wouldn't start watching any new soap operas if I were you."

"This is the most unusual complaint, Mrs. Quilch. Have you had it before?"

"Yes, doctor."

"Well, you've got it again!"

A man rushed into the doctor's office, jumped on the doctor's back, and began shouting "One! Two! Three! Four."

"Wait a minute!" yelled the doctor, struggling to free himself. "What do you think you're doing?"

"Well, doctor," said the eccentric man, "they said I could count on you!"

"What seems to be the trouble then, Mr. Worryalot?" asked the psychiatrist.

"It's like this, doctor," said the patient. "I have a huge mansion in the country, two Rolls-Royces, my children go to the most exclusive private schools, and my wife is dressed by the finest designer in Paris."

"So what's the problem?"

"I only earn $100 a week!"

"I don't think much of that new doctor."

"Why not?"

"Old Charlie Evans went to see him the other week. He tapped Charlie's knee with that little hammer and his leg fell off!"

"The trouble is," said the entertainer to the psychiatrist, "that I can't sing, I can't dance, I can't tell jokes, I can't act, I can't play an instrument or juggle or do magic tricks or do *anything*!"

"Then why don't you give up show business?"

"I can't—I'm a star!"

"One of my uncles was a doctor, but he gave it up."

"Why?"

"He just didn't have the patients."

"Doctor! Doctor! I feel like a racehorse!"

"Take these pills every four laps."

"Doctor! Doctor! I feel like a bee."

"Buzz off—I'm busy, too!"

"Doctor! Doctor! I've eaten a pencil! What should I do?"

"Use a pen."

"Doctor! Doctor! I'm a burglar!"

"Have you taken anything for it?"

"Doctor! Doctor! I keep seeing double."
    "Sit on the couch, please."
    "Which one?"

"Doctor! Doctor! I think I'm a dog."
    "Sit down, please."
    "Oh no—I'm not allowed on the furniture."

"Doctor! Doctor! I think I'm a telephone."
    "Take these pills and if they don't work give me a ring."

"Doctor! Doctor! I think I'm shrinking!"
    "You'll just have to be a little patient."

The wife of a man with a wooden leg called the doctor and said, "My husband has broken his wooden leg, doctor. Can you give him another one?" The doctor did, but a week later she called again. "My husband has broken his new wooden leg, doctor," she said. "Can you give him another one?" The doctor thought this was rather careless of the one-legged man, but he agreed to supply yet another wooden leg. But when the wife came in the following week for a new leg, and again the week after, he grew suspicious. "That's four new wooden legs your husband has had in the past month," he said. "What on earth is he doing?" "Oh, doctor," sobbed the wife, "I can't lie to you any longer. He's making a coffee table!"

"Doctor! Doctor! I feel like a ladder!"

"Keep calm and let me take it one step at a time."

A doctor was bothered by one of his patients who happened to live in the house next door. Whenever the patient felt sick he would bang on the wall; at two o'clock in the morning he would shout, "Doctor! Can you give me something for a headache?" At three o'clock in the morning he would shout, "Doctor! Can you give me something for a stomach ache?" At four o'clock in the morning he would shout, "Doctor! Can you give me something for arthritis?" Eventually the patient died, and the doctor thought that at last he would have some peace, but unfortunately he died only a week or two later. And as luck would have it the doctor was buried right next to his complaining patient, and on the night of his burial there came a knock on the side of his coffin and a voice called out, "Doctor! Can you give me something for worms . . . !"

A woman went to a doctor complaining of a twig growing out of her head. The doctor examined the growth and gave her some pills. Two weeks later she returned — the twig had grown to a branch with leaves and acorns on it. Again the doctor examined the growth and gave her some pills. But two weeks later she again returned—by now the branch had grown into a sapling and for the third time the doctor gave her some pills. Three months later the woman returned to his office. Her head was sprouting a tree with leaves along with bushes, rocks, and a waterfall.

"Ah, now I know what it is!" said the doctor. "You've got a beauty spot!"

"Doctor! Doctor! I think I need glasses!"

"You certainly do, ma'am. This is a diner!"

Grab Bag

One late autumn evening two boys, who had collected a bag of chestnuts, decided to split them up in a graveyard. On their way in one of the boys dropped the bag and two of the chestnuts rolled out. "We'll get those later," he said, and they went in to divide up the remainder. As they were counting them a small girl happened to be crossing the graveyard, and to her horror she heard from behind a bush a voice say, "One for you, one for me. One for you, one for me!" In terror she rushed to the gate and bumped into a policeman. "What's the matter, little girl?" he asked, for she was obviously in great distress.

"Oh, Mr. Policeman!" she wailed, "there's ghosts in the graveyard, and they're splitting up the dead bodies! Listen!" And as she held a trembling finger to her lips they heard a voice say, "One for you, one for me. And don't forget those two by the gate!"

"My girlfriend's got a twin."

"How can you tell them apart?"

"Her brother's got a beard."

"How do you do?"

"Do what?"

"Throw the baby down!" shouted the man to a woman on top of a blazing building.

"I can't!" she yelled back. "You might drop him!"

"No, I won't!" he shouted back. "I'm a professional goalkeeper!"

Reassured, the woman dropped her baby to the soccer player, who immediately bounced it three times and kicked it over the garden wall . . .

Paddy and Mick went duck hunting with their dogs but without any success. "I know what it is, Mick," said Paddy. "I know what we're doing wrong."

"What Paddy?"

"We're not throwing the dogs high enough."

Three cookies were crossing the street when the first one was knocked down; then the second was knocked down. What did the third cookie say as he reached the sidewalk in safety? "Crumbs!"

"What happens if my parachute doesn't open?" asked the trainee.

"You pull String A," said the instructor.

"But suppose that doesn't work?"

"You pull String B."

"But suppose *that* doesn't work either?"

"In that case," said the instructor with a smirk, "a great big hand comes down out of the sky, grabs you, and puts you down safe and sound. All right?"

The day dawned for the trainee to make his first parachute jump, and sure enough his chute failed to open. He pulled String A as instructed—nothing! He pulled String B—nothing! But then a great big hand came out of the sky, grabbed him and put him down safe and sound. And as he walked away a great big foot came down out of the sky and squashed him flat . . .

The inmates of a prisoner-of-war camp asked whether they could play a series of soccer games against their captors. "Certainly!" said the Camp Commander. "And everyone must practice hard! My men will practice on the bottom field, my officers will practice on the top field, and you prisoners will practice on the minefield!"

"Like to come to my birthday party on Saturday, Jill?"

"Thanks, Trevor. Where do you live?"

"Thirty eight London Road. Just push the bell with your elbow."

"Why with my elbow?"

"You're not coming empty handed, are you?"

POSTMAN: "Is this letter for you, sir? The name is all smudged."
MAN: "No, my name is Allsop."

"Dark in this cave, isn't it?"
  "Dunno—I can't see."

Did you hear about the farmer's boy who hated the country? He went to the big city and got a job as a shoeshine boy, and so the farmer made hay while the son shone!

A stranger walked into a bar and ordered a large brandy for himself and drinks for everyone in the bar. "And have one yourself," he said grandly to the bartender. Half an hour later the order was repeated: a large brandy for himself and drinks for everyone in the bar—and one for the bartender. He carried on like this all evening, every half hour ordering drinks all round—and one for the bartender, who eventually became concerned about the size of the bill. So when the stranger attempted his ninth gigantic order the bartender said, "I hope you won't mind my mentioning it, sir, but your bill now amounts to $168.75."

  "Does it?" said the stranger. "Well, I'm sorry to hear that, because I haven't got a penny on me!"

  The bartender leapt over the counter in a fury and grabbed the stranger by the throat; he slapped him in the face, kicked him in the shins and finally threw him out

28

through the door where he landed in a heap in the gutter.

The following evening the bar had only been open a few minutes when who should come in but the stranger! "A large brandy for me," he said, "and drinks for everyone in the bar. But I'm not giving you one," he said to the astounded bartender. "After a couple of drinks you get very nasty!"

"Imagine you're on a hike," said the Scoutmaster to Eric the Tenderfoot, "and you're facing north. Now, what is on your right?"

"East, Sir," said Eric.

"Correct. And what is on your left?"

"West, Sir."

"Correct again. And what is at your back?"

"Um—my backpack, Sir."

Sign in store window:

FOR SALE
Pedigree Bulldog.
House trained. Eats anything.
Very fond of children.

Advertisement in newspaper:

WANTED
Boy to trace gas leaks with
lighted candle.
Must be willing to travel.

"How old were you on your last birthday?"

"Nine."

"I see. So you'll be ten on your next birthday."

"No, I won't. I'll be eleven."

"How can that be?"

"I'm ten today."

"That girl looks like Helen Green."

"She looks even worse in red."

"There's a man outside with a big bushy beard."

"Is it a naval beard?"

"No, it grows on his chin."

Two boys were watching television when the gorgeous face and figure of Bo Derek appeared on the screen. "If I ever stop hating girls," said one to the other, "I think I'll stop hating her first."

"I've got over 5,000 records."

"Over 5,000! Gosh, you must be very fond of music."

"Oh, I don't play them. I just collect the holes in the middle."

"What steps would you take," roared the sergeant, "if one of the enemy came at you with a bayonet?"

And a small voice in the rear rank muttered, "Great *big* ones!"

"Why were you late back to camp, Frank?" asked the Scoutmaster.

"I'm sorry, Skip," replied the Scout. "But as we crossed that field of cows my beret blew off and I had to try on forty before I found it."

An old soldier was visiting the site of one of his past battles. "I remember this spot so vividly," he said to his wife, his eyes misting over with nostalgia. "It was here that my Captain fell."

"What he shot?" she asked gently.

"No. Blind drunk as usual."

FLYING INSTRUCTOR: "Tomorrow you will fly solo."
TRAINEE PILOT: "How low?"

"Yesterday my sister threw pepper in my face."

"Golly! What did you do?"

"Sneezed."

How do you stop a cold from going to your chest?

Tie a knot in your neck.

"This morning," said one pilot to the other, "I made a perfect three-point landing."

"That's nothing," came the reply. "This morning I made a perfect one-point landing."

"How did you manage that?"

"I got stuck on the church steeple!"

"My neighbors bang on the wall at all hours."

"Doesn't that keep you awake?"

"No, but it certainly interferes with my trumpet practice!"

"Is this Cohen, Cohen, Cohen, and Cohen?"

"Yes, madam."

"May I speak to Mr. Cohen, please? It's very important."

"I'm afraid Mr. Cohen is on vacation."

"Oh . . . may I speak to Mr. Cohen, then? It's extremely urgent."

"I'm afraid Mr. Cohen is out sick."

"Oh, dear . . . what about Mr. Cohen? It's a matter of life and death!"

"Mr. Cohen is in Brussels on business."

"Oh, Lord, I'm desperate! Can I speak to Mr. Cohen, then?"

"Speaking."

"Why are you jumping up and down?"

"I've just taken my medicine and I forgot to shake the bottle."

"This morning my Dad gave me soap flakes instead of cornflakes for breakfast!"

"I bet you were mad."

"Mad? I was foaming at the mouth!"

"Did you hear about Charlie Evans' diet? The doctor said he could only have bananas and coconut milk. For three months that was all he had—bananas and coconut milk!"

"Did he lose any weight?"

"No, but can he climb trees!"

"Some girls think I'm handsome," said the young Romeo, "and some girls think I'm ugly. What do you think, Sheila?"

"A bit of both. Pretty ugly."

"Why are you covered with bruises?"

"I started to walk through a revolving door and then I changed my mind."

The hit parade:
She Left Her Electric Blanket On, and Now She's the Toast of the Town
Don't Throw the Cat in the Washer, Mother, or You May Get a Sock in the Puss
They're Moving Father's Grave to Build a Sewer
Meet Me Under the Clothesline, Darling, 'Cause That's Where I Hang Out
Vesuvius Please Don't Blow Your Top, or, Lava Come Back to Me

"You have to be a good singer in our house, you know."
"Why's that?"
"There's no lock on the bathroom door."

Did you hear about the woman who dreamed she was chewing her pillow?

She was fine in the morning, just a little down in the mouth.

"Is it possible to eat soup politely with a big moustache?"

"Yes, but it's a big strain."

"I'd like to buy a dog."

"Certainly, sir. Any particular breed. An Irish setter, perhaps?"

"No, not an Irish setter."

"A Golden Labrador?"

"No, not a Golden Labrador. I don't want a colored dog. Just a black and white one."

"Why a black and white one, sir?"

"Isn't the license cheaper?"

As the fire engine pulled away from the station with its siren blaring—DA! *Da!* DA! *Da!* DA! *Da!*—the crew became aware of a boy running alongside it. The fire truck accelerated, surging through the traffic—DA! *Da!* DA! *Da!* DA! *Da!*—but still the boy managed somehow to keep up. Eventually the driver turned on to a highway where he could accelerate, but still the boy was there running alongside!

Mile after mile the fire engine tore along—DA! *Da!* DA! *Da!* DA! *Da!*—but the boy miraculously kept pace with the speeding vehicle. His superhuman running finally unnerved the driver, who, despite the urgency of the call, slowed and stopped. "Hey, kid!" he shouted to the boy who had also stopped. "What in blazes do you want?"

"An ice cream cone, please," came the reply, "with sprinkles!"

A lady in a bar noticed a man in the corner of the bar rapidly getting drunker and drunker. "I've seen you in here before," she snapped at him, "and you're always drunk. Why do you drink so much?"

"'Cause o' my problem, lady," he said mournfully as he downed another double Scotch.

"And what problem do you have, may I ask?"

"I drink too much."

"You're ugly!"

"And you're drunk!"

"Yes, but in the morning I'll be sober!"

Good news! I've been given a goldfish for my birthday ... the bad news is that I don't get the bowl till my next birthday!

Good news! At school today there will be free Coca-Cola for everyone ... the bad news is that the straws are 50¢ each!

Good news! My Dad's just bought me a great model train ... the bad news is that he forgot to buy the track!

A man who couldn't stop himself from stealing asked a doctor for help and advice.

"Try these pills," said the doctor. "They should help."

"But what if they don't?" asked the wretched patient.

"Then try to get me a VCR, will you?"

1ST ESKIMO BOY: "Where's your Mom come from?"
2ND ESKIMO BOY: "Alaska."
1ST ESKIMO BOY: "Don't bother—I'll ask 'er myself."

The new Boy Scout was asked by his father whether he had learned how to tie any knots.

"Oh, yes, Dad," replied the enthusiastic Scout. "And next week we're going to learn how to untie the Scoutmaster!"

"Last winter during the dark nights I dressed all in white so that the traffic would see me."

"Did that keep you safe?"

"No. I got knocked down by a snowplow."

"Young man," said the old lady to the Boy Scout, "can you see me across the road?"

"I don't know," replied the boy. "I'll go and find out."

"When's your birthday?"
    "August 26th."
    "What year?"
    "Every year."

Why is a tree surgeon like an actor?
    'Cause he's always taking boughs.

Which burns longer—a black candle or a white candle?
    Neither. They both burn shorter.

"That new restaurant has an interesting item on the menu."
    "Oh—what's that?"
    "Soup in a basket!"

Advertisement in the window of a dry cleaner:
    WE'LL CLEAN FOR YOU. WE'LL PRESS FOR YOU.
                WE'LL EVEN DYE FOR YOU.

Advertisement in the window of a drug store:
    GOT A COLD? TRY CHESTO COUGH DROPS.
    WE GUARANTEE YOU'LL NEVER GET BETTER.

Why did the golfer wear an extra pair of pants?
In case he got a hole in one.

SPORTS FAN: "I know you lost ten to nothing but why did you have to hit that little boy?"
BALLPLAYER: "He's our good luck mascot!"

"Want to try some of this? I've just invented it."
  "What is it?"
  "My new truth drink. One sip and you tell the truth."
  "All right, I'll try it . . . ugh! That's oil!"
  "And that's the truth!"

"Do you like this dress? It's seventy years old!"
  "Did you make it yourself?"

A boy riding his bicycle knocked over an old lady; she wasn't hurt, just shaken up and furious. "You wretched boy!" she fumed, dusting herself off. "Don't you know how to ride that bike?"
  "Yes," he replied, "but I don't know how to ring the bell!"

Which Senator has the biggest head?
   The one with the biggest hat!

Why did the cowboy die with his boots on?
   'Cause he didn't want to stub his toes when he kicked the bucket.

What did the judge say to his wife when he came home?
   "It's been another trying day."

What does a boy do when he wears his pants out?
   Wears them in again.

How many famous people were born in Denver?
   None—only babies.

"Even when my pocket's empty I've still got something in it."
   "What's that?"
   "A hole!"

"Do you like my new swimming pool?"

"It's marvelous. Must have cost you a fortune!"

"Yes, it did."

"But why isn't there any water in it?"

"I can't swim."

A man at the movies left his seat to buy popcorn. When he returned he said to an old lady sitting at the end of the row, "Did I step on your toe just now?" "You certainly did!" she said crossly. "Oh, good," came the heartless reply, "this is my row."

The woman in a theater box office was surprised one evening just before the show by the behavior of a patron. He bought a ticket, went away, and then returned a few minutes later to buy another one; he went away again, returned and bought a third ticket. Then he went away yet again, returned yet again and bought a fourth ticket. By this time the show had started, so the woman in the box office said, "I hope you don't mind my asking, sir, but why do you keep coming back and buying more tickets?"

"Every time I try and get into the theater," the hapless patron replied, "some guy takes my ticket and tears it in half!"

TELEPHONE OPERATOR: "Is that the lunatic asylum?"
SUPERINTENDENT: "Yes, but we're not on the phone."

"I'm holding a match and a lighter. Which is the heavier?"
  "The match of course."
  "No, 'cause they're both lighters!"

Two Irishmen looking for work saw a sign which read
TREE FELLERS WANTED. "Oh, now, look at
that," said Paddy. "What a pity dere's only de two of
us!"

A man went into the Post Office with some jelly stuck in
one ear and some chocolate cake stuck into the other. The
man behind the counter said, "Why have you got jelly in
one ear and cake in the other ear?" To which the customer
replied, "You'll have to speak up—I'm a little deaf!"

What do vegetarian cannibals eat?
  Swedes . . .

The convicted murderer was about to be shot. "Do you have any last request?" asked the prison warden. "Yes," replied the criminal, "I'd like to sing a song." "Very well," said the warden, and the condemned man began to sing: "Nine hundred and ninety-eight thousand, three hundred and twenty-eight bottles of beer on the wall . . ."

"This watch," said the snob, "is shockproof, waterproof, antimagnetic, and will work perfectly for one hundred years. I paid no less than $400 for it!"

"Did you really?" said his humble friend. "I bought a watch ten years ago for no more than 50¢; two days after buying it I dropped it in the river and it's been running nonstop ever since."

"The watch?"

"No, the river!"

"Are your teeth checked?"

"No, sort of off-white . . ."

"Why are you so angry?"

"It's all the rage."

Sign in stationery store window:

CALENDARS AND DIARIES
ALL WITH 1 YEAR GUARANTEES

Mr. Grouch was enraged when young Joe from next door began throwing stones at his greenhouse. "I'll teach you, you little punk!" roared the furious neighbor. "I'll teach you to throw stones at my greenhouse!"

"I wish you would," said the laughing boy. "I've tried three times and I haven't hit it yet!"

One very hot day an extremely small man went into a café, put his newspaper on a table and went to the counter. But on returning with his cup of tea he saw that his place had been taken by a huge, bearded, ferocious-looking man weighing 250 pounds and six feet nine inches tall. "Excuse me," said the little man to the big man, "but you're sitting in my seat."

"Oh, yeah?" snarled the big man. "Prove it!"

"Certainly. You're sitting on my ice cream."

"Why do you keep doing the backstroke?"

"I've just had lunch and I don't want to swim on a full stomach!"

Jemima's new shoes were too squeaky for the irritable librarian, and as Jemima tiptoed past the "Silence" sign the librarian yelled out, "*QUIIIIEEEEEETTTT!*"

"I'm collecting for the old folks' home. Do you have anything to contribute?"

"Hang on and I'll get Grandpa."

I wouldn't say Robert is stingy but every time he takes a quarter out of his pocket George Washington blinks . . . and he's so suspicious! He doesn't even trust himself—both his eyes watch each other all the time.

"I don't think these photographs you've taken do me justice."

"You don't want justice—you want mercy!"

Claude isn't exactly stupid, but when he went to a mind-reader he got his money back.

"I understand you buried your cat last week?"

"Had to. She was dead."

The private detective was reporting to his boss. "I traced the woman to Manhattan, sir," he said, "but then she gave me the slip. Then I traced her to Newark, and again she gave me the slip. I picked up her trail in Albany, where she again gave me the slip."

"This is getting monotonous, Holmes," said the boss. "What happened then?"

"I found her in Binghamton, sir and there—"

"She gave you the slip?"

"No, sir. In Binghamton she gave me the skirt."

Did you hear about the rock singer who got his shoelaces tangled up in his hair? When he stood up he broke his neck.

"There's a leaky roof in my office."

"Won't the landlord repair it?"

"Repair it? He's so cheap he's charging me an extra $5 a week for the use of the shower!"

Did you hear about the tragedy at the supermarket? A customer was leaning over the frozen-food counter when five fish fingers reached up and strangled him.

"*What's that awful ugly thing on your shoulder?*"

"I don't know—what is it?"

"Your head."

Why did the stupid man fall out of the window?
  He was trying to iron his curtains.

Why did the stupid man fall out of the tree?
  He was trying to sweep up the leaves.

Did you hear about the woman who was so cheap she
kept a fork in the sugar bowl . . . ?

After many years of searching, the wicked Abanazar finally found the magic cave which he hoped would contain
the wonderful lamp, the lamp that would make him master
of the universe. He stood before the rock that sealed the
entrance to the cave, spread his arms wide, and in a com-
manding voice said "Open Sesame!" And from within the
cave a ghostly voice answered, "Open says-a who?"

Two boys camping out in a backyard wanted to know the
time, so they began singing at the tops of their voices.
Eventually a neighbor threw open his window and shouted
down at them, "Hey! Keep it down! Don't you know
what time it is? It's three o'clock!"

"Tell me," said the hiker to the local yokel, "will this path take me to the main road?"

"Nope," replied the rustic, "you'll have to go by yourself!"

"I didn't come here to be insulted!"

"No? Where do you usually go?"

"No, no, no!" said the enraged businessman to the persistent salesman. "I cannot see you today!"

"That's fine," said the salesman. "I'm selling eyeglasses!"

A very grand lady made her first visit to a post office— previously one of her servants had always gone for her, but on this occasion curiosity got the better of her, and in she went to purchase a postage stamp. Gazing at the small gummed piece of paper she said haughtily to the clerk,

"Have I got to stick this on myself?"

"No, lady," came the reply. "You stick it on the envelope!"

Two trucks, one carrying a load of red paint and the other a load of purple paint, crashed on a desert island. The drivers are now marooned.

A man just released from prison was so elated after five years behind bars that he ran down the street shouting, "I'm free! I'm free!" And a small boy on the corner said, "So what—I'se four!"

Mr. Timpson noticed his neighbor, Mr. Simpson, searching very hard for something in his front garden. "Have you lost something, Mr. Simpson?" asked Mr. Timpson. "Yes," replied Mr. Simpson. "I've mislaid my glasses." "Oh dear," said Mr. Timpson. "Where did you last see them?" "In my living room," said Mr. Simpson. "In your living room?" asked Mr. Timpson. "So why are you looking for them in your garden?" "Oh," replied Mr. Simpson, "there's more light out here!"

CUSTOMER: This restaurant must have a very clean kitchen.
MANAGER: Thank you, sir. What makes you say that?
CUSTOMER: Everything tastes like soap!

"Do you know the quickest way to the station?"
"Yes—run!"

Think of the numbers two, four, seven, and eight . . . now, close your eyes . . . dark, isn't it?!

A woman who was seven feet tall and sixty inches wide worked behind the counter of a candy store. What did she weigh? Candy.

Charlie and Farley saw two men at a bridge fishing in a most peculiar manner. One was holding the other over the side by his ankles and the second was hooking the fish out of the water with his hands! Strange though this angling technique may have been it was remarkably successful, and the man being held over the bridge was throwing up big fish every few seconds. "Let's try that!" said Charlie to Farley, and Farley agreed. So on they walked till they came to another bridge, where Charlie held on to Farley's ankles and waited for his friend to throw up lots of fish. But five minutes went by and Farley had caught nothing; ten minutes, twenty minutes—an hour, then two hours, and still no fish. Then suddenly Farley called out, "Charlie, pull me up quick! There's a train coming!"

But Charlie let go of Farley, who was run over by the train and seriously injured. "Charlie!" yelled out Farley, "don't just stand there. Call me an ambulance!" "All right," said Charlie. "You're an ambulance!"

"What are you doing with that manure?" said the city boy to the gardener. "I'm putting it on my strawberries," replied the gardener. "Really?" said the city boy. "Where I live we put cream on them!"

Two men went to the employment office looking for work. The first was told he would be given a simple test of his abilities. "Who is the president?" he was asked. "Er—Abraham Lincoln," he replied. "Sorry that's wrong," said the clerk. "It's Ronald Reagan."

Outside the man said to his friend, "They'll ask you the president's name," he said. "I'll write it down for you and pin it inside your jacket." So in went the second man and again the clerk said, "Who is the president?" The second man looked inside his coat and answered, "Macy's!"

A man arrived home after eating at a restaurant to find that his home had been visited by burglars who had completely stripped the house—not a piece of furniture was left, no carpets, not so much as a light bulb remained! Furious at the loss, the man decided the restaurant was to blame. Accordingly he returned to the restaurant, stuck a gun under the manager's nose, and demanded the contents of the register. "Oh, surely, sir," said the manager calmly, "your meal wasn't that bad?"

Three men visited a wizard's castle to ask for help. "If you can spend one hour in my horrible dungeon," the wizard replied, "you will be granted your heart's desire. But you have one wish each, and only one, so choose carefully." The first man went in to the horrible dungeon, to find his nostrils assailed by the most awful, vile smell he had ever experienced. Doing his best to ignore the stench he concentrated on his wish—"I want to be a doctor! I want to be a doctor!" And sure enough after an hour he emerged a doctor. The second man entered and also managed to think safely of his heart's desire despite the terrible smell. "I want to be a lawyer! I want to be a lawyer!" And he too emerged after an hour a fully qualified lawyer. But when the third man entered he immediately said "Pooh!" and straightaway was turned into a bear. . . .

NEWSFLASH: 1,000 Wigs stolen in Miami. Police are combing the area.

Why did the lady have her hair in a bun?
    'Cause she had her nose in a cheeseburger!

How do you define agony?

A man with one arm hanging from a cliff with an itchy behind!

NEWSFLASH: Eminent plastic surgeon dies. He sat on a radiator and made a complete pool of himself.

Did you hear about the idiot stuntman who tried to jump over two dozen motorcycles in a bus? He might have succeeded but someone signaled for a stop.

Two children were admiring the famous statue of Rodin entitled "The Thinker." "What do you suppose he's thinking about?" said one, to which the other replied, "I'd say he's thinking about where he put his clothes!"

Stan had bravely climbed a tall tree but found himself unable to get down. "Why don't you come down the same way you went up?" his friend called out.

"No way!" Stan shouted back. "I came up head first!"

"How's your new guitar?"

"Oh, I threw it away."

"Why?"

"It had a hole in the middle!"

Tarzan had climbed to the top of a mountain in the middle of the amazon jungle. At the summit he was immediately surrounded by hideous monsters, ghouls, and demons of every kind. Do you know what he said? "Boy, am I in the wrong joke!"

The workmen had just finished laying a huge wall-to-wall carpet when one of them noticed a small lump right in the middle. "Oh, those must be my cigarettes," he declared. "I was wondering where they were." So rather than take up the carpet and go through the difficult process of relaying it he simple took a large mallet and knocked the lump down. Just then the lady of the house came in, carrying a tray. "I've brought you some coffee," she said. "And I think one of you left these cigarettes in the kitchen . . . oh by the way, have any of you seen my little boy's hamster?"

Two friends were out hunting grouse. A bird suddenly flew out of the bushes right before their eyes; one of the men raised his gun and fired. The grouse uttered a despairing squawk, its wings folded and it fluttered to the ground. "You didn't have to shoot it!" said the other man. "The fall would have killed it!"

In the swimming meet the first high diver announced that he would attempt a triple somersault with one and a half twists. The second diver arrived on the top board carrying a fish. "And what are *you* going to do?" asked the judge. The diver answered, "A somersault with pike!"

I Say! I Say!

What did the bull say after his famous visit to the china shop?
   "I've just had a smashing time!"

What did the boy candle say to the girl candle?
   "Let's go out together!"

What did one eye say to the other eye?
   "Between you and me, something smells!"

What did the girl magnet say to the boy magnet?
   "I find you very attractive."

What did the big clock hand say to the little clock hand?
   "I'll be back in an hour."

What did the egg say to the blender?
   "I know when I'm beaten."

What did the calculator say to the bank teller?
   "You can count on me."

What did the chick say when she came out of the shell?
   "What an egg-sperience!"

What did the Daddy Shoe say to the Baby Shoe?
   "You'll do in a pinch!"

What did the girl bulb say to the boy switch?
   "Boy, do you turn me on!"

What did the Baby Corn say to the Mother Corn?
   "Where's Pop Corn?"

What did one angel say to the other angel?
  "Halo there!"

What did the picture say to the wall?
  "First they frame me and then they hang me!"

What did the mother crow say to the nestling?
  "If you gotta crow, you gotta crow!"

What did the young porcupine say to the cactus?
  "Is that you, Daddy?"

What did one elevator say to the other elevator?
  "I think I'm going down with something!"

What did one tonsil say to the other tonsil?
  "You'd better get dressed——the doctor's taking us out tonight!"

What did one wall say to the other wall?
  "I'll meet you at the corner."

What did the dog say to the cat?
  "Woof Woof!" (What else?!)

What did the orange say to the lemon?
  "Hello, lemon . . ."

What did one flea say to the other flea?
  "Shall we walk or take a cat?"

What did the boy octopus say to the girl octopus?
  (Sing) "I wanna hold your hand, your hand, your hand, your hand . . . !"

What did the bald man say to the comb?
  "I'll never part with you."

What did the salt say to the pepper after a fight?
  "Shake!"

What did the big fountain say to the little fountain?
  "You're too young to drink."

What did the beaver say to the tree?
    "It's been nice gnawing you."

What did the King Egg say to the Bad Egg?
    "I'm going to have you eggsecuted."

What did the Principal Egg say to the Pupil Egg?
    "I'm going to eggspel you."

What did the big faucet say to the small faucet?
    "You little squirt!"

What did the small faucet say to the big faucet?
    "You big drip!"

What did one witch say to the other witch when inviting her to supper?
    "You'll just have to take pot luck!"

What did one chimney say to the other chimney?
    "I'm going out tonight—can I borrow your soot?"

What did one sardine say to the other sardine?
  "Move over—you're squashing me!"

What did one ear say to the other ear?
  "Just between us we need a haircut."

What did the big bus say to the little bus?
  "You're too young to be driving."

What did the big fly say to the little fly after they were both caught in a flypaper?
  "This is a sticky problem!"

What did the woman with a bad cold say to the druggist?
  "I need a box of a-a-atishoos!"

What did one chick say to the other chick when it found an orange in their nest?
  "Look at the orange Mama laid!" (Orange Marmalade)

What did the little eye say to the big eye?
   "Aye, aye, Captain!"

What did one flea on Robinson Crusoe's knee say to the other flea on Robinson Crusoe's knee?
   "Bye for now—I'll see you on Friday!"

What did the toothpaste say to the toothbrush?
   "Give me a squeeze and I'll meet you outside the tube."

Martini Hand Is Frozen

Knock! Knock!

—Who's there?
Adolf.
Adolf who?
A dolf ball hid me in de moud and I can't dalk dormal!

—Who's there?
Soup.
Soup who?
Soup-erman!

—Who's there?
Cows.
Cows who?
Cows go "moo" not "who"!

—Who's there?
Bet.
Bet who?
Bet you don't know who's knocking on your door!

—Who's there?
Juno.
Juno who?
Juno what time it is—my watch is broken?

—Who's there?
Europe.
Europe who?
Europe early this morning.

—Who's there?
Arfur.
Arfur who?
Arfur got.

—Who's there?
Egbert.
Egbert who?
Egbert no bacon.

—Who's there?
Luke.
Luke who?
Luke through the keyhole and you'll see.

—Who's there?
Ken.
Ken who?
Ken I come in?

—Who's there?
Bella.
Bella who?
Bella not-a work so I knock-a on-a de door!

—Who's there?
Dismay.
Dismay who?
Dismay be a joke but it doesn't make me laugh!

—Who's there?
Toby.
Toby who?
Toby or not to be . . .

—Who's there?
Rupert.
Rupert who?
Rupert your left arm in, your left arm out . . .

—Who's there?
Dawn.
Dawn who?
Dawn leave me standing out here in the cold. *Or (Sing)*
Dawn let the sun go down on me . . .

—Who's there?
Capfitz.
Capfitz who?
Capfitz you not who.

—Who's there?
Amos.
Amos who?
Amosquito.

—Who's there?
Anna.
Anna who?
Annather mosquito.

—Who's there?
Dishwasher.
Dishwasher who?
Diswashn't de way I shpoke before I had falsh teeth!

—Who's there?
Martini.
Martini who?
Martini hand is frozen so let me in!

—Who's there?
Zephyr.
Zephyr who?
Zephyr de doctor, I got a code id de node.

—Who's there?
Owl.
Owl who?
Owl you know unless you open the door?

—Who's there?
Wendy.
Wendy who?
(*Sing*) Wendy red, red robin comes bob, bob, bobbin'
along . . .

—Who's there?
Sal.
Sal who?
(*Sing*) Sal-ong way to Tipperary. . .

—Who's there?
Phyllis.
Phyllis who?
Phyllis up with a glass of water—I'm thirsty.

—Who's there?
Aardvark.
Aardvark who?
(*Sing*) Aardvark a million miles for one of your smiles, my Mammy. . .

—Who's there?
Noah.
Noah who?
Noah good place to eat?

—Who's there?
Police.
Police who?
Police let me in—it's cold out here!

—Who's there?
Mickey.
Mickey who?
Mickey's stuck in the door!

—Who's there?
William.
William who?
William mind your own business!

—Who's there?
Mary.
Mary who?
Mary Christmas.

—Who's there?
One.
One who?
One-der why you keep asking that?

—Who's there?
Howard.
Howard who?
Howard you like to stand out here in the cold while some idiot keeps saying "Who's there . . . ?"

—Who's there?
Max.
Max who?
Max no difference—just open the door!

Law and Disorder

The policeman in a patrol car was astounded to see, as he overtook a fast-moving car, that the woman at the wheel was knitting. He wound down his window and yelled, "Pull over!" "No," she called back. "A pair of socks!"

Seeing a woman standing helplessly by her car in a remote part of the countryside, the kindly policeman stopped and asked what was the matter. "Oh, thank you, officer," she said. "I've got a flat tire. I've managed to change the wheel, but now I can't lower the jack." "Very good, ma'am," said the policeman. "I'll see what I can do." "Please lower the car gently," said the woman. "My husband's asleep in the back seat!"

The policeman had brought a suspect in to the station and was smugly reporting his triumph to the sergeant.

"Good work, Plod," said the sergeant. "Has he got a record?"

"Oh, yes, Sarge," said the cop. "He's got three Adam Ants and a pile of Elton John's . . ."

"I'll have to give you a ticket, sir," said the traffic cop to the speeding driver. "You were doing eighty-five miles an hour." "Nonsense, officer," declared the driver. "I've only been in the car for ten minutes!"

"Why were you speeding, ma'am?" asked the traffic cop.

"Well, officer," came the reply, "my brakes are bad and I wanted to get home before I had an accident."

"Last year I opened a jeweler's shop."

"Any good?"

"No. He caught me at it."

The only way a policeman could quiet a rowdy drunk was to clonk him on the head with his stick. "What was that?" said the drunk. "It's just struck one," said the policeman. "Phew!" said the drunk. "It's a good thing I wasn't here an hour ago!"

"Last week in my store a man helped himself to three cans of peaches, the cash register and a pair of pants!"

"Didn't you chase after him?"

"No—they were my pants!"

"Stick 'em down!" snarled the fierce thief.

"Huh?" said the startled man.

"I said stick 'em down!"

"Don't you mean stick 'em up?"

"Oh—no wonder I'm losing money!"

Do you know what happened to the crook who stole the calendar? He got twelve months . . .

The criminal mastermind found one of his gang sawing the legs off his bed. "What are you doing that for?" demanded the boss.

"Only doing what you ordered," said the stupid thug. "You told me to lie low for a bit!"

Why did the police go to the seafood restaurant?

"Cause they'd had a report of fish being battered."

Why did the peanut complain to the police?
  'Cause he'd been assaulted.

"No trouble with the football fans this week, Sarge."
  "Why's that?"
  "The Giants are out of town!"

"Now as I understand it, sir," said the policeman to the motorist, "you were driving this vehicle when the accident occurred. Can you tell me what happened?"
  "I'm afraid not, officer," replied the motorist. "I had my eyes shut!"

A crook dashed into a Chinese restaurant, brandished a sawed-off shotgun under the manager's nose, and said, "I want everything you've got in the register!" To which the manager inscrutably replied, "To go?"

A murderer sitting in the electric chair was about to be executed. "Have you any last request?" asked the prison chaplain.
  "Yes," replied the wretched killer. "Will you hold my hand?"

At three o'clock in the morning a policeman came across a suspicious character skulking down a side street carrying two suitcases. "What's in the suitcase?" he demanded, pointing to one. "That's sugar for my tea!" said the man. "And what's in that suitcase?" asked the policeman, pointing to the other. "That's sugar for my coffee!" replied the man, whereupon the policeman hit him on the head with his stick. "What's that for?" said the man, rubbing his skull. "That's a lump for your cocoa!"

A jeweler standing behind the counter of his shop was astounded to see a man come hurtling through the window head first. "What on earth are you doing?" he demanded. "I'm sorry," said the man. "I forgot to let go of the brick!"

Two petty crooks had been sent by the Big Boss to steal a vanload of goods from a bathroom supplier. One stayed in the van as lookout and the other went into the store-room. Fifteen minutes went by, then half a hour, then an hour—and no sign of him. The lookout finally grew impatient and went to look for his partner in crime. Inside the store the two came face to face.

"Where have you been?" demanded the worried lookout.

"The boss told me to take a bath," came the reply, "but I can't find the soap and towel!"

Lines for Loonies

Don't eat school lunches,
Just throw them aside.
A lot of kids didn't,
A lot of kids died.
The meat's made of iron,
The fries are of steel,
And if *they don't* kill you,
The pudding will!

(To the tune of "Frère Jacques")
School lunches! School lunches!
Concrete fries! Concrete fries!
Tapioca pudding! Tapioca pudding!
I feel sick—bathroom quick!

(To the tune of "My Darling Clementine")
Build a bonfire! Build a bonfire!
Tie the teachers to the stake;
Put the Principal in the middle,
Then watch the whole bunch bake!

We go up and we go down,
We don't care if the school falls down;
No more English,
No more French,
No more sitting on the old school fence.
If the teacher interferes,
Tie her up and slap her ears;
If that doesn't serve her right,
Blow her up with dynamite!

Row, row, row your boat,
Gently down the stream;
Throw the teacher overboard,
Then you'll hear her scream!

Children are here buried in bunches,
Who died after eating public school lunches.

Doctor Bell fell down the well,
And broke his collarbone;
A doctor should attend the sick,
And leave the well alone!

There once was a great big cat,
who swallowed a whole baseball bat;
He swallowed the ball,
    The bases, gloves and all—
So the players knocked him flat!

Here comes the bride,
Sixty inches wide;
Look at her now as she wobbles,
Up the centre aisle.
Here comes the groom,
Biting his nails in gloom,
He's looking as thin as a dressmaking pin,
And never again will he smile.

There once was an old man of Wheeling,
Who had an expectorant feeling.
But a sign on the door,
Said DON'T SPIT ON THE FLOOR,
So he looked up and spat on the ceiling.

Little birdie flying high,
Dropped a message from the sky.
"Oh," said the farmer wiping his eye,
"Isn't it lucky cows don't fly!"

Latin's a dead language,
As dead as dead can be;
It killed off all the Romans,
And now it's killing me!

Monkey Business
And Other Beastly Jokes

We call our dog Carpenter 'cause he's always doing little odd jobs around the house.

What happens when the frog's car breaks down?
    He gets toad away.

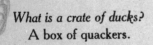

What is a crate of ducks?
    A box of quackers.

Why do cats and dogs turn around and around before sleeping?
    Because one good turn deserves another.

What do people in Mozambique call little black cats?
    Little black kittens.

What is a musical fish?
    A piano-tuna.

What does a frog do with bad eyesight?
    Hops to the hoptician.

Why are wolves like playing cards?
    They both come in packs.

Why did the whale let Jonah go?
    He couldn't stomach him.

How can you get a set of teeth put in for free?
    Hit a tiger.

What did the goat say when he only had thistles to eat?
    "Thistle have to do."

If a peacock lays an egg in your garden, who owns the egg?

No one—peacocks don't lay eggs, only peahens.

How do you shoe a horse?

Say "Giddy-up!"

Where does a two-ton gorilla sit when he goes to a movie?

Anywhere he wants to!

"We had roast boar for dinner last night."

"Was it a wild boar?"

"Well, it wasn't very pleased."

Where do you find wild boar?

Depends where you leave them.

What was the tortoise doing on the motorway?

About 150 yards an hour.

What is the animal with the highest intelligence?

A giraffe.

Why can't you trust an Indian leopard?
  'Cause it's a cheetah.

What happened at the badly organized milking contest?
  There was udder chaos.

Why was the camel unhappy?
  'Cause it had the hump.

Why are skunks always arguing?
  'Cause they like to raise a stink.

What animal are you like when you take a bath?
  A little bear.

*If there are five partridges in a pear tree and a hunter shoots
three, how many are left?*
  None — the others flew away.

If twenty dogs run after one dog, what time is it?
  Twenty after one.

A man walked into a bar with a huge, vicious looking Alsatian. "Sorry, sir," said the bartender, "but that dog looks dangerous to me. You'll have to leave him outside." So the Alsatian owner took his dog outside, then came back into the bar and ordered a drink. He was just finishing when a young woman came in and said, "Whose Alsatian is that outside?"

"Mine," said its proud owner.

"I'm afraid," said the young woman, "that my dog's just killed him!"

"Killed him!" said the man in disbelief. "What kind of dog do you have?"

"A Chihuahua," said the young woman.

"But how could a little Chihuahua kill my enormous Alsatian?"

"She got stuck in his throat and choked him."

A woman bought two parrots, one of whom she was warned was extremely aggressive. And it was, too! When she took the cover off the cage the morning after bringing them home the aggressive parrot had killed the other! To teach it a lesson, she bought a condor—and when she took the cover off the cage the next morning the parrot had killed it. Determined not to be beaten the woman bought an eagle! In the morning she took the cover off—and there was the eagle, dead on the floor of the cage! But this time the parrot had shed all its feathers! It stood on its perch, totally featherless, cocked its head on one side, looked at its owner and said, "I really had to take my coat off to take care of that one!"

Why can't you play jokes on snakes?
　'Cause you can never pull their legs.

A man standing at a bus stop was eating a hot dog. Next to him stood a lady with her little dog, which became very excited at the smell of the man's food and began whining and jumping up at him. "Do you mind if I throw him a bit?" said the man to the lady. "No, not at all," she replied. Whereupon the man picked up the dog and threw him over a wall . . .

Which shop do sheep like to visit?
　The baaaber's!

What's worse than a crocodile with toothache?
　A centipede with corns.

What's the definition of a caterpillar?
　A worm with a fur coat.

The loudmouthed frog said to the giraffe, "What do you eat, Mr. Giraffe?" "Leaves," said the giraffe. The loudmouthed frog then said to the antelope, "And what do you eat, Mr. Antelope?" "Grass," said the antelope. So the loudmouthed frog then said to the crocodile, "And what do you eat, Mr. Crocodile?" "Loudmouthed frogs," said the crocodile, to which the loudmouthed frog replied, (*with your mouth tightly shut*) "Oh, you won't see many of those around here!"

Why do bees hum?
    'Cause they don't know the words.

A man buying a camel was told that to make it walk he should say "Few," to make it run he should say "Many!," and to make it stop he should say "Amen!" At his first ride all went well. "Few!" he called, and off the camel went. "Many!" he shouted, and the camel began to run —straight for the edge of a cliff. But the new owner had forgotten the word to make the camel stop! As the cliff edge came closer and closer he called out in terror, "God save me! God save me! Amen!" And of course the camel stopped—right on the very edge of the cliff. The rider mopped his brow in relief and said, "Phew, that was clo-AAAAGH!"

Two fish were swimming in a stream when it began to rain. "Quick!" said one fish to the other, "Let's swim under that bridge, or we'll get wet!"

A family of tortoises went into a store for some ice cream. They sat down and were about to start when Father Tortoise said, "I think it's going to rain. Junior, will you go home and get my umbrella?" So off went Junior Tortoise for his father's umbrella, but three days later he still hadn't returned. "I think, dear," said Mother Tortoise to Father Tortoise, "we'd better eat Junior's ice cream before it melts." And a voice from the door said, "If you do that I won't go!"

What does a cat turn into when the lights go out?
   The dark.

"Who's been eating my porridge?" squeaked Baby Bear.
   "Who's been eating *my* porridge?" growled Father Bear.
   "Don't get so excited," said Mother Bear. "I haven't made it yet!"

"Who's been eating my porridge?" squeaked Baby Bear.
   "Who's been eating *my* porridge?" cried Mother Bear.
   "Burp!" said Father Bear...

Oh, No!

What did Lot do when his wife turned into a pillar of salt?
  He put her in a shaker.

What kind of lights did Noah have on the ark?
  Floodlights.

Why do actors hang around pool halls?
  'Cause they're sure to get some cues.

What kind of umbrella does a Russian carry when it's raining?
  A wet one!

Why was the baby raised on cat's milk?
　'Cause it was a baby kitten.

What is yellow, soft, and goes around and around?
　A long-playing omelette.

What is the shortest bridge in the world?
　The bridge of your nose.

What did the French Chef do when a customer fainted?
　Gave her the quiche of life.

Is censorship a good thing or not?
　It depends on whether the result makes censor not.

When are circus acrobats needed in restaurants?
　When tumblers are required on the tables.

If we get honey from a bee, what do we get from a wasp?
　Waspberry jam.

Why did the scientist have his phone cut off?
    'Cause he wanted to win the Nobel prize.

Why is it called the Eiffel tower?
    'Cause from the top you sure get an eyeful!

What would you say to a German barber?
    "Good morning, Herr Dresser!"

Why was Cleopatra so negative?
    She was Queen of denial.

What is the definition of a minimum?
    A woman with only one child.

What is a cow that eats grass?
    A lawn mooer.

What is purple and 4,000 miles long?
    The Grape Wall of China.

Why did the Lone Ranger take a hammer to bed?
  So he could hit the hay.

Who was Mexico's most famous fat man?
  Pauncho Villa.

What will happen to you at Christmas?
  Yule be happy.

What clothes do lawyers wear in court?
  Lawsuits.

What's rich and goes putt putt?
  A sunburned golf pro.

What is big, has four wheels and flies?
  A garbage truck.

Why did the antelope?
  Nobody gnu.

Why should business people remember Elijah's parents?
Because they made a prophet.

Why did the father call two of his sons Edward?
'Cause two Eds are better than one.

What do you call someone who steals pigs?
A ham-burglar.

What did Queen Guinevere say when she fell in love?
"Arthur any more at home like you?"

Did Cain hate his brother for ever?
No, just as long as he was Abel.

What is black and white and has eight wheels?
A nun on roller skates.

Where was chicken first fried?
In Greece.

How did the glowworm feel when it backed into a fan?
  Delighted.

What did the guests sing at the Eskimo's party?
  "Freeze A Jolly Good Fellow..."

What is the definition of "debate"?
  It's something dat lures de fish.

What is Shakespeare's most popular play in the Orient?
  Asia Like It.

What will a wise man say on the Last Day?
  "Armageddon out of here..."

What is yellow and goes click-click?
  A ballpoint banana.

What is Santa Claus's wife called?
  Mrs. Claus.

What did Mrs. Claus say to her husband during the storm?
   "Come and look at the reindeer."

Do sailors go on safaris?
   Not safaris I know.

What's big, hairy, and can fly?
   King Kongcorde.

What has a horn and drives?
   A car.

What lives in a pod and is a Kung Fu expert?
   Bruce Pea.

Why are you tired on April Fool's Day?
   'Cause you've just had a thirty-one days' March.

Why are adults boring?
   'Cause they're groan-ups.

What do cannibal children like playing best?
　　Swallow my leader.

What do Eskimos use for money?
　　Popnickles.

How do sheep stay warm in winter?
　　Central bleating.

Why did Henry VIII have so many wives?
　　He liked to chop and change.

What kind of cans are there in Mexico?
　　Mexicans.

How would you describe a stick of rhubarb?
　　A stick of celery with high blood pressure.

Why did the fireman wear red trousers?
　　His blue ones were at the cleaners.

Why are goldfish gold?
  So they won't get rusty.

What is a mermaid?
  A deep-she fish.

"Why are you taking that steel wool home?"
  "I'm going to knit myself a car."

Did you hear about the stupid waterpolo player?
  His horse drowned . . .

Did you hear the joke about the roof?
  It's way over your head.

What happened to the idiot who sat on the floor?
  She fell off.

Did you hear about the stupid tap dancer?
  He fell in the sink.

Why did the bald man look out of the window?
   To get some fresh air.

Where does Tarzan buy his clothes?
   At a Jungle Sale.

What did Tarzan say when the tiger started chewing on his leg?
   aaAAAAAAAAaAAaAAa! (*Give Tarzan yell*)

Why did the orange stop rolling down the hill?
   It ran out of juice.

Who makes suits and eats spinach?
   Popeye the Tailorman.

Preserve wildlife—pickle a squirrel.

If King Kong went to Hong Kong to play ping pong and died, what would they put on his coffin?
   A lid.

When a lemon calls for help, what does it want?
  Lemonade.

If you drop a white hat into the Red Sea, how does it come out?
  Wet.

What's green and white and bounces?
  A spring onion.

How do you make gold soup?
  Use fourteen carats.

Where do bees go for a ride?
  The buzz-stop.

What's white and climbs trees?
  A refrigerator—I lied about it climbing trees.

What's white and blue and climbs trees?
   A refrigerator wearing blue jeans. (And I'm still lying about it climbing trees.)

What vegetable plays pool?
   A cue-cumber.

How do ghouls eat?
   By gobblin'.

How do you cut through the waves?
   With a sea-saw.

Do robots have brothers?
   No, only tran*sisters*.

Why do some women wear curlers at night?
   So they can wake up curly in the morning.

What rock group kills household germs?
   The Bleach Boys.

What do miners play in the tunnels?
  Mine-opoly.

What's yellow and goes around and around?
  A banana in a washing machine.

What happened to the man who dreamed he was eating a giant marshmallow?
  When he woke up his pillow had disappeared.

What happened to the man who slept with his head under the pillow?
  When he woke up he found the fairies had taken all his teeth out.

What do you call a cucumber that insults the farmer?
  A fresh vegetable.

Why couldn't the sailors play cards?
  'Cause the captain was standing on the deck.

What's black and white and extremely difficult?
   An SAT exam.

What did the policeman have in his sandwiches?
   Traffic Jam.

Why did the rooster cross the road?
   To show he wasn't chicken.

How do you take a sick pig to the hospital?
   In a hambulance.

Where do you take a sick dog?
   To the dogtor.

What do you get if you give sugar and egg whites to a monkey?
   Meringue Outan.

What does a pig use to write his letters with?
   Pen and oink.

We all know that a nun rolling down a hill goes black-and-white-and-black-and-white, but what is black and white and goes ha-ha? The nun that pushed her!

What was Beethoven's favorite fruit? (Sing to the opening four notes of Beethoven's Fifth Symphony:)
  Banana-*naaaa*!

Have you heard the joke about the dog that walked twice from New York to Los Angeles?
  No, neither have I . . .

What's a good place for waterskiing?
  A sloping lake.

Where would you find a stupid shoplifter?
  Squashed under Macy's.

Who invented fire?
  Some bright light . . .

What fish are other fish most scared of?
    Jack the Kipper.

What would you call a freight train loaded with candy?
    A Chew-Chew train.

What goes "Click-click—have I done it?"
    A blind man doing the Rubik Cube.

What jacket is always burning?
    A blazer.

What makes a tree noisy?
    Its bark.

Why is a bee's hair always sticky?
    'Cause it uses a honeycomb.

What do you get if you drop a piano on an army camp?
    A flat major.

What happened to the hyena who swallowed a bouillon cube?

He made a laughing stock of himself.

What do frogs drink?

Croaka Cola.

Where would you weigh a pie?

(Sing) Somewhere over the rainbow, weigh a pie . . . (way up high!)

Why didn't the banana snore?

'Cause it was afraid to wake up the rest of the bunch.

What looks like half a loaf of bread?

The other half.

Who is the biggest gangster in the sea?

Al Caprawn.

What do you call ants who run away very fast to get married?

Ant-elopers.

What does Luke Skywalker shave with?

A laser blade.

Did you hear about the idiot who had a brain transplant?

The brain rejected him!

Why did the idiot have his sundial floodlit?

So he could tell the time at night.

What do you do with a gas leak?

Put a bucket under it.

If you want to know where the sun goes after it sets, just stay up all night and finally it will dawn on you!

What's yellow and leaps from cake to cake?
　Tarzipan.

What's the fastest thing in water?
　A motorpike.

Hear about the world's worst athlete? He ran a bath and came in second.

What's very intelligent and loves boating?
　A row-bot.

Where do snowmen go to dance?
　A snowball.

How did the Mother Banana spoil the Baby Banana?
　She left him in the sun too long.

Which capital city cheats on exams?
　Peking.

What do you call a flea that lives in an idiot's ear?
    A space invader.

Why did the woman take a bale of hay to bed?
    To feed her nightmare.

What do cats prefer for breakfast?
    Mice Crispies.

What do ants take when they are sick?
    Antibiotics.

Where do astronauts park their space ships?
    On meet-eorites.

What's black and white and noisy?
    A zebra with a drumkit.

What's big, has wheels, and lies on its back?
    A dead bus.

What's yellow and goes slam-slam-slam-slam?
   A four-door banana.

Why did the idiot jump out of the window?
   To try out his new spring suit.

Why did the idiot spring out of the window?
   To try out his new jump suit.

Did you hear about the indecisive Kamikaze pilot?
   He flew ninety-nine missions . . .

How do you kill a cheapskate?
   Throw a nickel under a bus.

Did you hear about the terrorist who tried to blow up a bus?
   He burnt his lips on the exhaust pipe.

What's black and white and bounces?
   A penguin on a pogo-stick. *Or* a rubber nun.

What do you call a sleeping heifer?
    A young bulldozer.

Shall I tell you the joke about the postcard that hadn't been stamped? No, you'd never get it.

The Old Jokes
at Home

"*Why is your brother called cotton?*"
  'Cause he shrinks from washing!"

"*Any luck with your advertisement for a husband?*"
  "Yes, I've had sixteen answers. And they all say the same thing."
  "What's that?"
  "You can have mine!"

Why did the comedian's wife sue him for divorce?
  He kept trying to joke her to death.

"My Dad's in the hospital. Last week he went down to the garden to cut a cabbage for our dinner. The knife slipped and he stabbed himself."

"Gosh! What did your Mom do?"

"Opened up a can of peas."

"Mommy, may I leave the table?"

"Well, you certainly can't take it with you!"

Despite his big brother's warnings, little Jasper insisted on walking along the top of a high wall. "Well," said big brother, "if you fall and break both your legs, don't come running to me!"

"Daddy, I don't like cheese with holes."

"Just eat the cheese and leave the holes on the side of your plate."

"Grandma, what's a weapon?"

"A weapon is something you fight with."

"You mean like Grandpa?"

Sandra and Simon were arguing over the breakfast table. "Oh, you're stupid!" shouted Simon. "Simon!" said their father, "that's quite enough of that! Now, say you're sorry."

"All right," said Simon. "Sandra, I'm sorry you're stupid."

"Is your brother fat?"

"I'll say! He's so fat he had mumps for three weeks before we found out!"

"Why were you born in Boston?"

"'Cause my mother wanted me near her."

Why was the Egyptian girl worried?

'Cause her Daddy was a Mummy.

Why did Grandpa put wheels on his rocking chair?

'Cause he wanted to Rock'n'Roll.

"Katie, have you finished your alphabet soup?"

"Not yet, Mom. I'm only up to the Ks . . ."

Little Helen and her Mommy were at the movies. After half an hour or so, Helen whispered "Mommy, is your seat comfortable?" "Yes, thank you, dear," replied her mother. "Can you see the screen all right?" "Yes, thank you, dear." "Are you sitting in a draft?" "No, dear." "Then can I change places with you?"

"Mommy, I don't want to go to France!"
    "Shut up and start swimming . . ."

"Mommy, why can't we have a garbage can like everyone else?"
    "Shut up and keep eating."

The family seated in a restaurant had finished their dinners when Father called the waiter over. "Yes, sir?" said the waiter.

    "My son has left a lot of meat on his plate," explained Father. "Could you give me a bag so that I can take it home for the dog?"

    "Gosh, Dad!" exclaimed the excited boy. "Do we have a dog now?"

Did you hear about the three daughters in the kitchen?

One washed up, one dried up, and the third picked up the pieces.

"Mrs. Finnegan!" said her neighbor crossly. "Have you told your son to stop imitating me?"

"Yes, I've told him to stop acting like a fool!"

"Stephen, it's time for your violin lesson."

"Oh, fiddle!"

"Stephen, it's time for your drum lesson."

"Oh, smashing!"

LITTLE BROTHER: "Look, Sis, I've got a pack of cards."

BIG SISTER: "Big deal!"

For her tenth birthday Jessica received a bottle of perfume and a tape player. Two old friends of her parents came to dinner that night, and as she sat between them at the table she confided, "If you hear a little noise and smell a little smell—it's me!"

"Steve, you've been fighting again, haven't you?"

"Yes, Mom."

"You must try to control your temper. Didn't I tell you to count up to 10?"

"Yes, but Vic's Mom only told him to count up to five so he hit me first!"

Amos asked his mother if they could have a VCR.

"I'm afraid we can't afford one," sighed his mother.

But the next day Amos came in, staggering beneath the weight of a brand-new VCR.

"How on earth did you pay for that?" gasped his mother.

"Easy, Mom," replied Amos. "I sold the television!"

Why did Henry put a frog in his sister's bed?

'Cause he couldn't catch a mouse.

A man whose wife died instructed the stonemason to carve on her headstone the words "She Was Thine." But when he went to inspect the result the mason had put "She Was Thin." The grieving widower angrily informed the artisan that he had left an E out. "Sorry," said the stonemason, "I'll fix it, never fear. I'll put the E in tomorrow." But when the widower went to see the tombstone the legend now read, "E, She Was Thin . . ."

"And do you like your new school?" asked grandmother fondly.

"Well, sometimes, Granny," said little Jacob.

"When?"

"When it's out!"

"What does your Dad do?"

"He's a government artist."

"What does he draw?"

"Unemployment!"

Pix 'n' Puzzles

What's this?

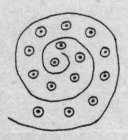

Fifteen Mexicans walking down a mountain path.

How can one plus one equal a window?

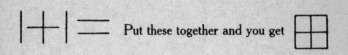 Put these together and you get

What's this?

A koala bear climbing up a tree.

What's this?

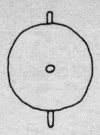

A Mexican riding a bicycle.

What's this?

A fountain pen nib.

Put down ten matches to make the word WET. How can you remove two matches yet still have a three-letter word? You simply remove the first two matches, leaving the word VET!

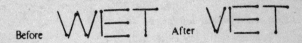

Before WET   After VET

Say to a friend: Do you know Shakespeare's stamp? *Your friend will say "No" and you then say* Shake... *(shaking him by the shoulders)*...spear... *(spearing him)*... stamp! *(Stamping on his toe!)*

If it takes ten men four days to dig a hole, how long will it take five men to dig half a hole? There's no such thing as half a hole!

A boy wanted to cross a river from south to north; he couldn't swim, no boats were available, and the only bridge was watched over by a guard who came out of his hut every five minutes. Since it took ten minutes to walk across the bridge how did the boy achieve his goal?
Answer: He walked across from south to north; as the guard emerged from his hut the boy turned around and

pretended he was walking from north to south. The guard then ran after him and chased the boy back the way he thought he had come—i.e. to the north side of the river!

How can a rooster lay an egg on barbed wire?
   Roosters don't lay eggs; hens do!

If a man rides into an inn on Friday and stays three days, how can he ride out on Friday?
   Answer: Friday was the name of his horse!

A donkey wanted to cross a stream in order to eat the lush grass in the meadow opposite. There was no bridge, no boat, and the donkey couldn't swim. So how did he cross? . . . You give up? . . . So did the donkey!

Three boys called Peter, Paul, and Pardon went to play by the river. Peter and Paul fell in and were drowned: who was left? *(You will of course receive the reply "Pardon," at which you repeat loudly:)* Three boys called Peter, Paul, and Pardon . . . etc.

A motorist in his car with his two sons was in a crash. He and one of his sons were killed, and the other son was taken to a hospital, where the doctor said, "This is my son." How can this be?

Answer: The doctor was his mother.

In the school the backward children were placed in a classroom on the ground floor, the slow children on the first floor, the problem children on the second floor, and the real delinquents on the third floor. What was on the top floor?

The teachers' lounge!

A frog is lying on a lily pad in the middle of a pond. If he is six inches from the north edge, six inches from the south edge, and four inches from the east and west edges, where will he jump to get out of the pond?

He won't jump at all because he's dead.

I saw Esau sitting on a seesaw—how many S's in that?

There aren't any S's in THAT!

A man with a cat, a mouse, and a lump of cheese has to cross a river in a small boat, but he can only take one thing with him at a time. So how does he get them all across without the cat eating the mouse or the mouse eating the cheese?

Answer: First he crosses with the mouse, then he crosses with the cat and returns *with the mouse*, which he leaves behind while he crosses with the cheese, finally returning for the mouse!

If a red house has red bricks, a blue house has blue bricks, a black house has black bricks, and a pink house has pink bricks, what color bricks does a green house have? A greenhouse doesn't have bricks—only glass!

A diesel train enters a tunnel running due north-south. If the train enters the tunnel at the north end, which way does the smoke blow?

Diesel trains don't have smoke!

"What's five Q and five Q?"
   "Ten Q."
   "You're welcome!"

A man is in a prison cell with no doors and no windows; there are no holes in the ceiling or trapdoors in the floor, yet in the morning the guards find him gone. How did he get out?

Answer: Through the door*way*—there were no doors, remember?!

Is it "nine and five *is* thirteen" or "nine and five *are* thirteen"? Neither—nine and five are fourteen!

What was the tallest mountain in the world before Mount Everest was discovered?

Answer: Still Mount Everest—the fact that it was undiscovered makes no difference, it was still the highest mountain in the world.

If a dog is tied to a rope fifteen feet long, how can it reach a bone thirty feet away?

Answer: The rope isn't tied to anything!

How can you drop an egg three feet onto a concrete path without breaking it?

Answer: Drop it *four* feet. It will certainly be smashed, but only after dropping *more* than three feet!

"Did you hear about the fool who keeps going round saying No?"

"No."

"Oh, so it's you!"

In an apple-eating contest Sue ate ninety apples and Selena ate a hundred and one. How many more apples did Selena eat than Sue?

Answer: Ten—Selena ate a hundred and *won*!

Say to a friend "What's this?" Then wave your hand like a snake. Your friend will say "I don't know," so then you wave your other hand in a similar manner and say "Neither do I—but here comes another one!"

A man committed suicide by hanging himself from a high beam in a remote barn. There was no way to climb up to the beam, and the only thing the police found in the barn was a puddle of water beneath the body. How did he get up to the beam in order to hang himself?

Answer: He stood on a block of ice!

A deaf and mute man went into a hardware store to buy a hammer. He couldn't speak so he mimed hammering . . . then another deaf and mute man went in wanting a screwdriver, so he mimed putting in a screw . . . Then a blind man went into the store. He wanted a saw. So what sort of mime did he do?

He didn't mime at all—he just asked for it!

Two boys were born on the same day, on the same date, to the same set of parents. They look alike, talk alike, think alike and behave alike—yet they are not twins! How can this be?

Answer: Because they are two of a set of triplets!

Try this on a friend. Ask "Would you kiss a bum for $1?" The answer will of course be "No!" Then you ask "Would you kiss a bum for $5?" And again the answer will be "No!" You then ask "Would you kiss a bum for $10?" And for the third time the answer will be in the negative. But then you say, "What would you kiss a bum for?" The answer you receive this time will probably be, "Nothing." To which you reply, "Oh, so you'd kiss a bum for nothing, would you?!" Or the reply might be, "I wouldn't kiss a bum for anything!" to which you can respond, "So you would kiss a bum for something, then!"

"Why doesn't the President wave with this hand?" *(Wave your left hand)*

"I don't know. Why?"

"Because it's *my* hand!"

"Let's have a race to say the alphabet."

"All right."

"The alphabet—beat you!"

As I was going to St. Ives,
I met a man with seven wives.
Every wife had seven sacks,
Every sack had seven cats.
Every cat had seven kits—
Kits, cats, sacks, wives,
How many were going to St. Ives?
Answer: Only me—all the rest were coming *from* St. Ives!

"Which would you rather be——half-drowned or saved?"

"Saved, of course."

"But if you're only half-drowned you *are* saved!"

A tropical lily is growing in a pond. If it doubles its size every day and takes twenty-two days to fill the entire area of the pond, how far will it have reached on the twenty-first day?

Answer: Halfway—because it doubles its size every day!

What is frozen water? Ice.
What is frozen cream? Ice cream.
What is frozen tea? Iced tea.
What is frozen coffee? Iced coffee.
What is frozen ink? Iced ink. (I stink).
You'd better go and take a bath, then!

"You still owe me twenty cents for that honey."
  "What honey?"
  "I never knew you cared!"

If there are fifty-two weeks in the year, how many seconds are there?
Twelve—January 2nd, February 2nd, March 2nd, etc., etc.

Which month in the year has twenty-eight days? All of them . . .

What's your favorite color? Red? And what is your favorite animal? A cat? And what is your favorite number? Seven? So when did you last see a red cat with seven legs . . . ?!

If an airplane crashed on the border of England and Scotland, where would the survivors be buried?

Nowhere, 'cause the survivors wouldn't be dead!

Riddle-Tee-Hee

Why are 4,840 square yards like a bad tooth?
　Because it's an acre.

What is bought by the yard and worn by the foot?
　A carpet.

Why did the apple turnover?
　'Cause it saw the cheese roll.

What cakes do children dislike?
　Cakes of soap.

Why is it dangerous to put the letter "M" into the freezer?
  Because it changes ice into mice.

Why is the sea always restless?
  'Cause it's got so many rocks in its bed.

What did one toe say to the next toe?
  Don't look now but there's a big heel following us!

Why are your tonsils unhappy?
  'Cause they're always down in the mouth.

When is a student like a rope?
  When it's taut.

What's the best place to go to when you're dying?
  The living room.

How many coats can you get into an empty closet?
  Only one—after that it isn't empty!

Why are bridge players aggressive?
  'Cause they often lead with a club.

Where do you get satisfaction from?
  A satisfactory.

What question always receives the answer Yes?
  How do you pronounce Y E S?

Why did the milkmaid sit down?
  'Cause she couldn't stand milking.

Who is bigger: Mrs. Bigger or her baby?
  Her baby, who is always a Little Bigger.

Why does a young lady need the letter Y?
  'Cause without it she'd be a young lad.

How does a ship listen?
  Through its engineers.

What do you have when you don't feel well?
    Gloves on your hands.

Who earns a living without doing a day's work?
    A night watchman.

How can you always tell an undertaker?
    By his grave manner.

Why is your nose in the middle of your face?
    'Cause it's the (s)center.

Why is the sea so suspicious?
    'Cause it's been crossed so often.

How many balls of string would it take to reach the Moon?
    Just one HUGE one!

What is it that even the most careful person overlooks?
    His nose.

On which side of Jack's house did his Beanstalk grow?
  On the outside.

What goes up a chimney down but not down a chimney up?
  An umbrella.

What did the digital watch say to her mother?
  "Look, Ma! No hands!"

Why are there so few lady pilots?
  'Cause no girl wants to be a plane woman!

Why is perfume always very obedient?
  'Cause it is scent wherever it goes.

Why can the world never come to an end?
  'Cause it's round.

Why is the letter A like noon?
  'Cause it's in the middle of the day.

Why is an airplane like a con man?
    They both have no visible means of support.

What happened to the man who jumped off a bridge in Paris?
    He went in Seine.

Why did the weeping willow weep?
    'Cause it saw the pine tree pine.

How do barbers get to their shops quickly?
    They take short cuts.

Why are dentists unhappy?
    'Cause they're always looking down in the mouth.

Which word is always pronounced wrongly?
    The one that's spelled W R O N G L Y.

Why is the letter T an island?
    'Cause it's in the middle of water.

When were there only three vowels in the alphabet?
   Before U and I were born.

Why is the letter A like a flower?
   'Cause a B is always after it.

Why did the communist chicken cross the road?
   'Cause it was a Rhode Island Red.

What pet makes the loudest noise?
   A trum-pet.

What do you always take down when you're run over by a car?
   Its license plate.

Why did the cat cross the road?
   'Cause it was stapled to the chicken . . . (ugh!)

Where was Rosie when the lights went out?
   In the dark.

What lock went to a university?
  A Yale.

What flashes by but doesn't move?
  A telephone pole when you're traveling in a car.

Why was the Boy Scout dizzy?
  He'd done too many good turns.

What tune do you sing in a car?
  A car-toon.

What is full of holes but can hold water?
  A sponge.

What did the bell say when it fell in the water?
  "I'm (w)ringing wet!"

What makes the Tower of Pisa lean?
  It doesn't eat much.

Why are bakers wealthy?
   'Cause they make good dough.

Why did the rock singer go to the barber?
   He couldn't stand his hair any longer.

How do you get rid of varnish?
   Take away the letter R.

Which roof covers the noisiest tenant?
   The roof of your mouth.

What doesn't ask questions but has to be answered?
   A telephone.

What fish do dogs chase?
   Catfish.

What is open when it's closed and closed when it's open?
   A draw bridge.

If a crocodile makes shoes what does a banana make?
  Slippers.

What travels faster: heat or cold?
  Heat, because it's easy to catch a cold.

What travels around the world yet stays in one corner?
  A postage stamp.

What two kinds of fish are needed to make a shoe?
  A sole and an eel.

Did you hear about the red sauce chasing the brown sauce?
  It couldn't ketchup.

How many days of the week start with the letter T?
  Four: Tuesday, Thursday, today, and tomorrow.

What is a tornado?
  Mother Nature doing the twist.

What do you call a letter when it's dropped down the chimney?
Blackmail.

Why is a chemistry lesson like a worm in a cornfield?
They both go in one ear and out the other.

What runs and whistles but can't talk?
A train.

What jam can't be put on your bread?
Traffic jam.

What nail can't be hit with a hammer?
Your fingernail.

"Look, there's a nail!"
"Where?"
"On the end of my finger!"

What driver can't drive?
  A screwdriver.

What vegetable do you need a plumber for?
  A leek!

Have you heard the joke about the wall?
  You'd never get over it!

What's the biggest nut in the Army?
  The kernel.

Why did the rabbit cross the road?
  To show his girlfriend he had guts.

Why is a lion in the desert like Christmas?
  'Cause of its Sandy Claws.

What happens if you walk under a cow?
  You get a pat on the head.

What are the best things to put in an apple pie?
  Your teeth!

What has four eyes and a mouth?
  The Mississippi.

What gets bigger the more you take away?
  A hole.

What whistles when it's hot?
  A kettle.

How would you describe beans on toast?
  Skinheads on a raft.

What is the longest word in the dictionary?
  Elastic, because it stretches.

What runs around a garden without moving?
  A fence.

How does an octopus go into battle?
    Fully armed.

Why did King Kong climb up the Empire State Building?
    To catch a plane.

What is the principal part of a lion?
    Its mane.

What should you do if your nose goes on strike?
    Picket.

Who won the Super Bowl in 1966?
    No one—the first Super Bowl was held in 1967.

What is the best place for a party on board a ship?
    Where the funnel be.

What is the softest bed a baby can sleep on?
    Cot-on wool.

A barrel of beer fell on a brewery worker. Why wasn't he hurt?
    'Cause it was full of light beer.

What am I if someone takes away all my letters?
    A postman who's been mugged.

How can you avoid falling hair?
    Jump out of the way.

How can you knock over a full glass without spilling any water?
    Knock over a full glass of milk.

What can never be made right?
    Your left ear.

What can you make that can't be seen?
    A noise.

What is the best way to cover a cushion?
    Sit on it.

If twelve make a dozen how many make a million?
    Very few.

What do misers do when it's cold?
    Sit around a candle.
What do misers do when it's very cold?
    Light it.

What did the idiot do with a flea in his ear?
    He shot it.

*What is a container that hasn't any hinges but has a golden
treasure inside?*
    An egg.

*A little thing, a pretty thing, without a top or bottom. What
am I?*
    A diamond ring.

What is the fastest vegetable in the world?
  An electric bean!

What did the man say when he stepped on a candy bar?
  "I've set foot on Mars!"

What bow can't you tie?
  A rainbow.

How does a professional hypnotist travel?
  By public transportation.

What is the smallest ant in the world?
  An infant.

What is always behind time?
  The back of a clock.

Why should you always have plenty of clocks in the house?
  Because time is precious.

Why did the simpleton bury his car battery?
    'Cause the mechanic told him it was dead.

Why did the stupid postman get the sack?
    To put his stupid letters in.

Why was the United Nations worried when a waiter dropped his tray?
    'Cause it was the fall of Turkey, China was broken, and Greece was overthrown!

Rolling in the Aisles

"Father, come quickly! The church is on fire!"
"Holy smoke!"

"Don't you enjoy the sound of church bells?"
"Sorry?"
"I said 'don't you like the bells?'"
"Eh?"
"AREN'T THE BELLS WONDERFUL?"
"It's no good—I can't hear a word you're saying over those darned bells!"

Sunday School teacher: "Who sits at the right hand of God?"
Sunday School Student: "Er—Mrs. God?"

"I didn't see you in church last Sunday, Nigel. I hear you were out playing football instead."

"That's not true, Reverend. And I've got the fish to prove it."

Jemima had just returned from her first visit to Sunday School.

"Well, Jemima," asked her father, "did you learn much?"

"Not a lot," said the little one. "I've got to go back next week."

Young Oliver had heard a sermon in which the preacher, when talking about Man's origins and ultimate destiny, had used the Biblical phrase "Ashes to ashes, dust to dust." Oliver returned home and went up to his room; but a few minutes later he came running downstairs and yelled to his mother, "Mom—you'd better come upstairs!"

"Why, Oliver?"

"'Cause I just looked under my bed, and there's somebody either coming or going!"

Adam was naming all the animals. "And that," he said to Eve, "is a rhinoceros."

"Why call it a rhinoceros?" asked Eve.

"Because," said the First Man scornfully, "it looks like a rhinoceros, stupid!"

"My wife's an angel."

"Really? Mine's still alive."

A priest was appalled to find a small boy sitting at the back of the church playing rock 'n' roll on his harmonica. "That's quite enough of that!" said the priest sternly. "Don't you know the First Commandment?"

"No, Father," replied the boy, "but you hum it and I'll try to follow along!"

Sunday School teacher: "Hands up all those who want to go to Heaven? . . . Hands up . . . what about you, Terry? You haven't got your hand up—don't you want to go to Heaven?"

Terry: "I can't. My Mom told me to go straight home!"

Everyone in the Primary School was very excited over the forthcoming visit of the bishop. "Now I want you all on your best behavior," said the principal, "and if the bishop should address any of you children, you must speak up and call him Father."

The great day arrived and the saintly bishop beamed upon the assembled tots. To one little boy he said kindly, "And how old are you, my son?" Confused and overawed the boy gasped out, "Oh—er—My God, I'm six!"

A preacher was thrilled when a member of his congregation told him that his sermon had been like the peace and mercy of God. But the good preacher wasn't so pleased when he looked up the quotation in his Bible and found that it read: "The peace of God passeth all understanding and his mercy endureth for ever"!

An elderly pilgrim returning from Lourdes had arrived at Kennedy Airport, and on going through customs said that he had nothing to declare. "What's in this bottle?" asked the Customs officer.

"Oh, that's just holy water from the Lourdes spring," said the pilgrim. But the Customs officer sniffed the contents, dipped in his finger, and licked it.

"This isn't holy water," he said sternly, "it's whiskey!"

"St. Bernadette be praised!" declared the pilgrim piously, "another miracle!"

Mr. Smithers was a missionary, and was sent to a central African country. On arriving at his new post he sent a telegram to his wife in America. Unfortunately it was delivered by mistake to another Mrs. Smithers whose husband had died only the day before. Just imagine her horror when she opened the telegram and read: ARRIVED SAFELY THIS MORNING. THE HEAT IS AWFUL!

Two astronauts knocked on the Pearly Gates, and St. Peter answered. "Come in, gentlemen," said the Archangel. "Just sit down there while I look up your files."

"Oh, we don't want to come in," said the first astronaut.

"You don't?" asked the astonished St. Peter. "What do you want then?"

"Please, sir," said the second astronaut, "can we have our capsule back?"

Arriving at a small village the traveling preacher asked a little boy for directions to the local church. The boy duly gave him directions, and the preacher said, "Thank you, my son. I shall be giving a sermon in the church tonight and I'd like you and your Mommy and Daddy and all your friends to come."

"What for?" asked the urchin suspiciously.

"Because," explained the preacher, "I want to tell you all how to find Heaven."

"What a joke!" sneered the brat. "You didn't even know where the church was!"

"Father! Father!" said the young curate urgently to his parish priest. "There's an old man in a long white beard sitting at the back of the church—he says he's God! What should I do?"

"Go and keep an eye on him," said the older priest, "and try to look busy!"

The minister's son was watching his father preparing the sermon for next Sunday.

"How do you know what to say, Daddy?" he asked.

"God tells me," replied his father.

"Then why do you keep crossing things out?"

Little Susan was attending church for the very first time. "What are all those people doing?" she asked her mother.

"Sssh, dear!" replied her mother. "They're praying."

"What—with all their clothes on?!"

"Was old Reverend Prendegast a successful missionary?"

"Certainly. He gave the tribesmen in Mbabaland their first taste of Christianity."

Two ministers were talking, and one said, "I had a terrible experience last Sunday. Absolutely awful!"

"What was that?" his brother minister asked in concern.

"Well, I dreamed that I was in my pulpit preaching," said the first minister, "and when I woke up—I found that I was!"

Two comedians were talking, and one said, "I hear your agent got you a booking in the Vatican. Is that really true?"

"That's quite correct," said the other, "but I canceled."

"Canceled?" exclaimed the first comedian. "You canceled a booking to entertain the Pope and all the Cardinals?"

"Well, how would you like to do *your* act in Latin?"

"And I'm afraid this is goodbye, God," said the little girl as she finished her prayers. "We're moving tomorrow."

Of course, Cain wanted to be as popular as his brother, but he turned mean when he found out he wasn't Abel . . .

How does an airline pilot's child finish his prayers? "God bless Mommy, God bless Daddy, and God bless me. Over and out."

"Young Esmeralda, an avid television viewer, was taken to her first church service. When asked by her Granny how she had enjoyed it, she replied. "The music and the singing were all right, but I didn't like the News."

"Do you really believe Jonah was swallowed by a whale?"
    "When I get to Heaven I'll ask him."
    "But suppose he's in the Other Place?"
    "Then you ask him."

"It'd *better* rain," muttered the kangaroo to his companion as they entered the Ark. "We've hopped a long way for this."

"Brother Damien, why is the chapel bell ringing this morning?"
    "Because Brother Augustine is pulling the rope, you idiot!"

What does God have for his tea?
Angel cakes.

What's the easiest way to get to Heaven quickly?
Stand in the highway.

A little boy went to confession and said to the priest, "Father, I threw peanuts into the river." The priest couldn't see too much harm in that, so he gave the boy a light penance. Another boy entered the box and also said, "Father, I threw peanuts into the river." The priest was again puzzled, but not wishing to show his confusion sent the second boy away with a light penance. But in came another youngster—he'd thrown peanuts into the river as well—and another boy, and another! Then a very tiny child came in, and the priest said, "And I suppose you threw peanuts into the river?"

"No, Father," said the boy, "I *am* Peanuts!"

"How did the wedding go today?" the caretaker asked the minister's secretary.

"Not too well, I'm afraid," replied the secretary. "The minister's eyesight got him into trouble again."

"Oh, no!" exclaimed the caretaker. "What did he do this time?"

"He married the groom to the best man, kissed the statue of the Virgin Mary, and locked the bride in the offerings box!"

Little Amy was sent to church with two dimes—one to put in the collection plate and the other to buy herself candy. But crossing the road the little girl tripped, and one of the coins dropped out of her hand, rolled along the pavement—and fell down a grating!

"Sorry, Lord," she said as she picked herself up. "There goes your dime!"

The Salvation Army girl was in the saloon with her collection plate, which she rattled under the nose of the oldest man in the bar. "What's this for?" he growled.

"I'm collecting for the Lord," she said.

"You'd better give me the plate, then," he replied. "I'll be seein' Him before you, lady!"

A passionate preacher was in the pulpit; his voice rose in a great crescendo of triumph, then fell quavering in terror and pity. His arms flapped and flailed, his face glistened with fervor, the veins stood out upon his forehead, his eyes bulged, and his nostrils quivered with righteousness. In the front pew was a small girl attending her first sermon.

"Mommy," she whispered, having watched the fanatical preacher in growing alarm, "what will we do if he gets out?"

The airliner was forty thousand feet above the Atlantic when, to the passengers' horror, an announcement crackled from the cabin loudspeakers. "This is your captain speaking! I regret to say we have an emergency. Two of our engines have failed. I have every expectation of reaching our destination safely but in the meantime will you please extinguish your cigarettes and fasten your safety belts? Thank you." One of the passengers, who was sitting next to a minister, immediately flew into a panic. "Don't just sit there!" he screamed at his religious neighbor. "Do something religious!" So the parson took up a collection . . .

"I want to be good!" declared the penitent in the confessional. "Can you help me, Father?"

"Of course I can, my son," said the good priest comfortingly. "The Lord is merciful."

"Could you forgive someone who steals $30, Father?"

"Certainly, my son," said the priest, "but you must tell me all about this theft."

"Well," said the petty crook, "there was $10 from Woolworth's yesterday and $10 from K-Mart today."

"But that only makes $20."

"Oh, I'll be getting the other $10 from Sears tomorrow!"

A minister and a cabdriver both died at the same time, but to his chagrin the minister discovered that the cabbie had been sent to Heaven while he was consigned to the other place. "Why should this be?" the aggrieved clergyman complained to St. Peter. "After all, I must have prayed to the Lord far more than that cabbie."

"That may well be so," replied St. Peter. "However, each time you gave a service everyone fell asleep, but when that cabbie gave *his* service everyone prayed!"

In which Biblical story is tennis mentioned?
    When Moses served in Pharaoh's court . . .

SUNDAY SCHOOL TEACHER: Mavis, why should we pray for grace?
MAVIS: Er, 'cause she's a very bad little girl, Ma'am?

Thieves who broke into a church were terrified to hear, as they approached the vestry in search of gold plate, a deep voice saying, "I'm going to eat your arms . . . then your legs . . . then your head . . . and then your body!" With a shriek they hurtled back out through the window whence they had entered, tumbled down the ladder, and scurried off as fast as their legs would carry them. Meanwhile, back at the vestry, the chaplain was finishing the last of his favorite jelly bears. "I'm going to eat your arms . . ."

Did you hear about the little boy who was christened
Glug-Glug?

The priest dropped him in the bowl.

Report Cards

Why are teachers special?
  'Cause they're in a class of their own.

What happens to the girl who misses the school bus?
  She catches it when she gets home.

"Anna, who was the first woman?"
  "Don't know, Ma'am."
  "Come along, come along. It had something to do with an apple . . ."
  "Oh, yes, Ma'am. Granny Smith!"

"What did your teacher think of your homework?"

"He took it like a lamb."

"Really? What did he say?"

"Baa!"

Tommy was late for school yet again, this time coming out with a spectacularly lurid and transparently false excuse.

"Now then, Tommy," said his teacher, "do you know what happens to children who tell lies?"

"Yes, Ma'am," said the impertinent boy. "They become teachers!"

This year's class trip will be to the beach!	Hooray!
It will cost $40 . . .	Boo!
. . . by train or $1.50 on the bus!	Hooray!
The principal will be coming . . .	Boo!
. . . to see us off!	Hooray!
The weather will be wet and windy . . .	Boo!
. . . in Russia and warm and sunny in America!	Hooray!
There will be no swimming . . .	Boo!
. . . until we get there!	Hooray!
Lunch will be liver and spinach . . .	Boo!
. . . for me and cheeseburgers and fries and Cokes for you!	Hooray!
There will be a visit to the museum . . .	Boo!
. . . or if preferred to the park!	Hooray!
But we must be back by twelve o'clock. . .	Boo!
. . . at midnight!	Hooray!

"Sarah," said the teacher, "what is a cannibal?"

"I don't know, Ma'am."

"Well, if you ate your parents, what would you be?"

"An orphan, Ma'am."

"Mom, I don't wanna go to school! I don't wanna go to school!"

"Now, dear, you must go, and for two very good reasons. First, you're fifty-six years old and second you're the principal!"

"William, why are you late for school again?"

"Sorry ma'am, but I dreamed I was playing football and the game went into overtime!"

"Violet, can you spell banana for me?"

"Well, sir, I know how to start but I don't know when to stop."

"How old would you say I am, Francis?" the teacher asked.

"Forty, sir," said the boy promptly.

"You seem very sure," said the puzzled teacher. "What makes you think I am forty?"

"My big brother's twenty, sir," replied the boy, "and you're twice as dumb as he is!"

"Melanie!" said the teacher sharply, "you've been doing Rebecca's homework for her again! I recognized your handwriting in her workbook."

"No, I haven't, Ma'am," declared Melanie. "It's just that we both use the same pencil!"

"Jarvis—I hope I didn't see you copying just then . . . ?"

"I hope you didn't too!"

"Philip," asked the chemistry teacher, "what is HNO_3?"

"Oh, er . . . just a minute, Ma'am . . . er . . . it's on the tip of my tongue, Ma'am . . ."

"Well in that case—spit it out. It's nitric acid!"

"Theo, why were you absent from school yesterday?"

"Oh, er, I wasn't well, Ma'am. I had a temperature."

"I see. And do you have a note from your Mother or your Father?"

"No ma'am."

"I shall expect to see one tomorrow. Is that clear?"

"Yes. Ma'am."

Next day Theo handed in the following note: "Dear ma'am, Theo was absent from skool on Toosday on account of a cold. Yours faithfully, My Father."

"Selena, why are you late this time?"

"Sorry, sir, but I was walking along High Street when I saw a road sign that said Go Slow. So I did!"

What must you pay when you go to school?

Attention.

The principal was amazed at the improvement in work and behavior of his school's most notoriously unruly class —all the more so since a new teacher had taken over only that semester. "Well done, Miss Blenkinsop!" he said warmly. "But tell me, how do you keep your class on their toes?"

"Put tacks on their seats!"

A girl was sent home by an angry teacher for not wearing her school uniform. She returned half an hour later dripping wet. "What's the meaning of this?" demanded her teacher. "You told me to wear my school clothes," said the miserable pupil, "but they were in the wash!"

"Sir!" said Alexander. "Empty Coke cans, wax paper, plastic bag, used tissues, broken bottles, empty cardboard boxes—"

"Alexander!" snapped the teacher. "You're talking rubbish again!"

"Now Frank," said the weary math teacher, "if you had $7 in one pocket and $7 in another pocket, what would you have?"

"Someone else's pants on!"

"Ma'am! Ma'am!" cried little Jamie, "I just banged my fumb on the door!"

"Not 'fumb', Jamie," said the teacher. "It's *th*umb!"

"Yes, ma'am. And I banged my thinger as well!"

"Sir, you know you told us yesterday that a pound of feathers was the same as a pound of lead?"

"Yes, what about it?"

"My Dad said you were wrong. He said I should try tickling your toes with a pound of lead!"

I won't say our school lunches are bad but even the garbage cans have ulcers!

"Why are you home from school so early, Jackie?"

"I was sent home, Mom, 'cause the boy next to me was smoking."

"But if *he* was smoking why should *you* be sent home?"

"I set him alight!"

GYM TEACHER: "Alison, you're hopeless at sports. You'll never be first in anything."

ALISON: "I'm first every day in the lunch line, Ma'am!"

The first grade class had been told to draw a scene representing the flight into Egypt. One little boy proudly displayed a drawing of a jet containing the three members of the Holy Family—but also a fourth figure. "When I said 'flight' I didn't quite mean a jet," said the teacher. "However, we'll let that pass for now. But who is the fourth person on the plane?" To which the little boy replied, "That's Pontius Pilate!"

Andy came home from his first day at school crying. "What's the matter, Andy?" asked his worried parents. "It's the school lunch," he sobbed. "It was awful! I couldn't touch it, and I'm hungry!" "I'm sure it can't have been that bad," said his father. "What was the lunch?" "Worms and balls!" came the astounding reply. Andy's mother immediately telephoned the school and spoke to the principal. "Andy's very upset about today's school meal," she said. "Can you tell me what it was?" "Certainly," said the principal. "Spaghetti bolognaise!"

Paul was being bawled out in the principal's office. "Your teacher has been complaining to me about you," said the principal sternly. "What have you been doing?"

"Nothing, sir," said Paul miserably, to which the principal replied, "Precisely!"

"Philip, what does it mean when the barometer falls?"
    "Er—the nail's come out of the wall, ma'am?"

Stewart owned a very small newt of which he was extremely fond, so much so that he couldn't bear to be parted from it even when he was going to school. One day his teacher spotted him at his desk gazing intently into a matchbox. "What have you got there, Stewart?" demanded the teacher. "It's a newt, ma'am," replied the boy. "Why do you keep it in a matchbox?" asked the teacher, to which Stewart replied, "Because it's my newt!" (Minute)

At a school concert one of the teachers noticed that little Dorothy seemed unable to clap her hands—whenever she tried they kept missing each other. After the concert the teacher took Dorothy aside and tried to teach her how to clap properly, but without success. "You try and practice over the weekend," said the kindly teacher, "and if you can clap properly on Monday I'll buy you some ice cream."

So all over the weekend little Dorothy practiced hard, and on Monday she triumphantly displayed to the teacher her newfound powers of coordination.

"Well done Dorothy," said the teacher. "Come into the playground at break and I'll buy you some ice cream. And true to his promise at lunch the teacher bought Dorothy a huge cone which he handed to the little girl, who took it delightedly and went—(bring up your closed fist and bang it on your forehead) slap!

In the locker room after a football game the coach asked whether any of the boys had seen his glasses. "I saw them on the field, Sir," answered Harry.

"Well, why didn't you bring them in?" asked the teacher.

"I thought you didn't want them any more, Sir," said Harry, "so I stepped on them!"

"Gary, did your sister help you with this homework?"
"No, ma'am. She did it all!"

Shaggy Dog
Stories
And Other Tall Tails

Brother Benedict had been a monk for many, many years, and was delighted to be told by his Superior one day that he had a visitor. He rushed to the parlor and found that the caller was none other than an old friend from his schooldays. They were reminiscing happily when, deep in the cellars of the monastery, came a tremendous crash and a long, mournful howl. "What on earth was that?" asked the visitor, startled. "I'm sorry, Andrew," said Brother Benedict, "but I am bound to secrecy by my Holy Vows, and as you are not a monk I cannot tell you."

After another half an hour Andrew left, still puzzled by the subterranean mystery, and promising to visit his old friend should he ever happen to be in the vicinity again. But it was to be ten long years before he returned; ten long years before he was sitting again in the monastery parlor with Brother Benedict. "Now you can tell me what is going on in the cellars here," said Andrew, "for as you can see from my habit I have become a monk myself, and for ten long years I have wondered what caused that crash and that howl."

At this point you say "And do you know what caused the crash and the howl in the cellar . . . No? . . . Well, I can't tell you because you're not a monk!"

Conrad lived in a four-bedroom house. He went into the first bedroom where his father was busy decorating, and said, "Dad, I think you're putting that wallpaper up the wrong way." To which his father replied, "Who's decorating this room—you or me?" So Conrad went into the second bedroom of his four-bedroom house where his brother was making a model airplane. "Oliver," he said, "I think you're putting that wing on wrong." To which his brother replied, "Who's making this model—you or me?" So Conrad went into the fourth bedroom of his four-bedroom house—

At which point you will be asked, "But what about the third bedroom?" To which you reply, "Who's telling this story—you or me?"

There was once a fabulously wealthy man who lived far from civilization in a huge golden house. Everything in the house was gold—the bricks, the doors, the floors, the furniture, the knives and forks; everything that could possibly be gold was indeed of pure, finest quality gold. One night, as the fabulously wealthy man lay in his golden bed between his golden sheets, there came a ring on the golden bell. He rose, put on his golden bathrobe, walked down the golden passage to the golden stairs and down to the golden hall where he opened the golden door. "I'm sorry to bother you," said the stranger on the golden doorstep, "but my car has broken down and this seems to be the only house for miles and miles. Could you possibly put me up for the night?" "Of course," said the fabulously wealthy man, "follow me." And he took the stranger through the golden hall, up the golden stairs, and along the golden passage. "You may sleep here," he said, "in this golden bedroom. In the golden cupboard you will find a pair of golden pajamas. Sleep well."

The fabulously wealthy man returned to his golden bed and was just falling into a light doze when again the golden bell roused him. It was a second stranger whose car had broken down, and he was also shown to a golden bedroom. Similarly a third stranded stranger who rang the golden bell a half hour or so later was lodged in yet another golden bedroom.

In the morning the three travelers found themselves in a huge golden breakfast room. They sat at a vast golden table as a servant entered, wearing golden livery and a powdered golden wig. "What would you like for breakfast, gentlemen?" he asked. "Cornflakes or eggs?"

"I'll have cornflakes," said the first.

"I'll have cornflakes as well," said the second.

"I'll have eggs, please," said the third.

Which proves that two out of three people prefer cornflakes for breakfast . . .

(As you begin this story you say to your listener, "You're the bus driver, right? Don't forget.")

A bus carrying four passengers stopped at the first stop and five people got on; at the next stop six got off and ten got on; at the next stop one got on but nobody got off. At the next stop nobody got on but three got off; at the next stop the bus went straight past, to the consternation of an old lady who wanted to get off. However, at the next stop she did get off, and a couple got on. There was one more stop to go before the bus reached the end of the line; only one got on here, and at the end of the line of course everybody got off. Now, what was the bus driver's name?

(By this time your listener will have completely forgotten the beginning of the story and will invariably say, "I don't know." To which you reply, "Yours—you're the driver, remember!?")

On his eighteenth birthday Jeremy was given a beautiful Victorian pocketwatch by his father. "Take good care of it," said his father. "That's a family heirloom—my great-grandfather gave it to my grandfather, my grandfather gave it to my father, and now I am giving it to you. Good luck, my boy, and I hope I live long enough to see you hand it on to your son."

A few weeks later Jeremy was watching a stage show. The last act before the intermission was a magician, who asked for someone to lend him a watch. So up went Jeremy on to the stage where he handed over the precious gift. "Thank you," said the magician. "Now, watch carefully as I place this beautiful timepiece in this envelope . . . I seal it down . . . thank you."

The magician then produced a large hammer, placed the envelope on a table, and smashed the hammer down upon it with all his might! He pounded and pounded—and then paused: something had obviously gone wrong, for small wheels and cogs and springs and bits of metal were flying around in all directions—the watch was smashed to smithereens! Utterly beyond repair! Jeremy rushed off the stage, ran up the center aisle to the manager's office and burst in.

"That fool has smashed my watch!" he roared.

"Calm yourself, sir, please!" said the manager smoothly. "Do sit down. Would you care for a cup of coffee?"

But Jeremy was not so easily distracted. "Now look here, what about my—?"

"Do you take milk?" asked the manager.

"Oh, er, yes. Just a bit. But what about—"

"Sugar?"

"Yes. But what about—?"

"Here you are, sir," said the manager with a smile as he handed Jeremy the cup of coffee. And what do you think he handed Jeremy with the cup?

(Your listener is bound to say "The watch." To which you reply, "No—a brownie!")

The Chicago Kid loved to gamble for very high stakes. Unfortunately the Chicago Kid was also very unlucky, eventually losing his car, his house, his business, his family, his friends—everything. In his wretchedness he entered a church and fell to his knees.

"Just give me a big win tonight, Guardian Angel," he implored with tears running down his face, "and I swear I'll never gamble again." And to his astonishment he heard a small voice in his ear that said, "Very well, Kid. If you are sincere I'll help you. Just this once."

Overjoyed, the Kid rushed off to the casino where he stood at the roulette wheel, his last ten dollars in his trembling hand, waiting for guidance. "Put the ten dollars on Red Number Twelve!" said that small clear voice in his ear. Ashen-faced, the Kid did as his Guardian Angel instructed. The wheel was spun, the ball was thrown; it skipped and danced around the wheel and finally came to rest—in Red Number Twelve! The Kid had won! As he reached forward to pick up his winnings he heard again that small, clear voice. "Leave it there, Kid. Let it ride!" And the Kid obediently withdrew his hand, leaving his winnings still on Red Number Twelve.

With sweat running down his face and his knees knocking, the Chicago Kid watched the little silver ball again skipping and dancing around the spinning wheel. "In seconds," he thought, "all my worries will be over! I'll be rich!" And the little silver ball dropped neatly into— Red Number Thirteen! As the Chicago Kid, numb with horror, gazed incredulously at the now still wheel, the small, clear voice in his ear said, *"Darn . . . !"*

One wild and stormy winter's evening a young girl called Sandra was called by her mother. "Daddy and I have to go out for a couple of hours," she said. "Will you be all right on your own?"

"Of course I will, Mommy," said the self-possessed young lady, but after her parents had left, a sudden loud noise made her jump—but then she laughed to herself. It was only the telephone! However, when Sandra lifted the receiver, all she could hear was a gasping, eerie voice that said, "My name is Bloody Fingers! I am coming to your house! I'll be there in five minutes!"

With a terrified sob Sandra slammed the receiver down and ran up to the attic; she locked the door behind her, pushed a heavy trunk against it, and then crawled into the farthest, darkest corner of the attic and lay, shaking with fright, under an old carpet.

Scarcely had she reached this hiding place when the sound of crashing, splintering wood above the howling of the wind told the frightened girl that the front door had been broken open; she heard heavy, dragging footsteps coming along the hall and up the stairs. And then, to her unspeakable horror, the attic door was also forced open and the heavy trunk pushed aside! Peeping out from under the carpet, she saw dimly, by flashes of lightning, a huge, hideous, wild-eyed, shaggy-haired man lurching toward her. As he drew closer she saw—oh, horrible!—that both his hands were dripping with blood! "What do you want?!" she screamed.

And again she heard that awful, ghostly voice. "I am Bloody Fingers!" said the vile creature stretching out his hands toward her, "and please—could I have a Band-aid?"

After spending the evening in the local bar a man emerged at closing time to find a storm raging. The wind was howling and the rain was lashing down, so he decided to take a short cut through the churchyard. It was very dark and spooky walking between the gravestones with the thunder booming and the lightning crackling, but the man kept going—until, above the noise of the storm, he thought he heard a tapping sound. His curiosity getting the better of his nervousness he followed the sound until suddenly, by the glare of prolonged flashes of lightning, he saw this weird old man, dressed in what appeared to be a white sheet, tapping away at a headstone with a hammer and chisel. "What are you doing?" asked the man, his surprise mingled with terror.

"I'm fixing this headstone," said the creature. "They've spelled my name wrong . . . !"

A squid was swimming through the ocean when he met his friend Mr. Whale. "And how are you today, Mr. Squid?" asked Mr. Whale. "Oh, I'm not too well at all," said Mr. Squid gloomily. "I don't know what's the matter with me."

"Oh dear," said Mr. Whale sympathetically. "Why don't you take my advice? Whenever I'm feeling bad I always swim a little deeper. If I were you I'd go down fifty feet; I'm sure you'll feel better then."

"I don't think I can swim any deeper," replied Mr. Squid. "I'm not heavy enough."

"Well, let me help you," said the obliging Mr. Whale, and he pushed Mr. Squid down and down and down, when suddenly from behind a rock appeared Mr. Squid's archenemy, Mr. Shark!

"Hello, Mr. Shark," said Mr. Whale cheerily. "Here's that sick squid I owe you!"

One Saturday night a latecomer sidled into the Army camp a full fifteen minutes after his pass had expired. The sergeant asked for an explanation, and the soldier replied, "I tried to get a taxi, Sarge, but they was all busy. So I saw this guy with a horse and cart and offered him a fiver to give me a lift. But halfway up the hill the horse dropped dead, so I had to walk the rest of the way."

"Do you think I'm going to fall for a ridiculous story like that?" roared the sergeant. "You're under arrest! Lock him up!"

Just then another latecomer arrived at the camp gate. "And where do you think you've been?" demanded the sergeant ominously. "Well, Sarge, it was like this," explained the second soldier. "I couldn't find a taxi anywhere, but I spotted this geezer with a horse and cart and I offered him a fiver for a lift. But halfway up the hill the horse dropped dead so I had to walk."

"You bum!" yelled the orderly sergeant. "I've never heard such a crock! You're under arrest! Lock him up!" And as the cell door clanged shut behind the second latecomer a third arriving puffing out apologies.

"And I suppose you couldn't find a taxi, eh?" asked the sergeant heavily, tapping his highly-polished toe. "Oh, I got a taxi all right," came the reply.

"You did? Then why are you so late?"

"Couldn't get up the hill past all the dead horses."

Once upon a time were three little worms called Foot, Foot-Foot, and Foot-Foot-Foot. One day, as they were crossing the road to do their shopping, Foot was run over by a steam-roller and squashed flat. Terrible tragedy! Of course Foot-Foot and Foot-Foot-Foot were extremely upset, but a day or two after the funeral Foot-Foot said to Foot-Foot-Foot, "I know we've had an awful shock, but life goes on and we must still do the shopping."

"Yes, I suppose you're right," sighed Foot-Foot-Foot to Foot-Foot. "But we must be very careful. After all, we've got one Foot in the grave already!"

A traveler stranded miles from anywhere decided to spend the night in an old, creepy inn. "We have one room vacant," said the landlord, "which we don't usually rent. There is a trapdoor in the center of the room and I must ask you not, on any account, to open it. Do you understand? *Do not open the trapdoor!*"

Naturally the traveler agreed and was shown into the room, which seemed very comfortable—except for the trapdoor. He could not take his eyes off it, wondering what secret lay hidden below it. His curiosity finally got the better of him; he grasped the ring set into its center and slowly pulled. The trapdoor rose protestingly, and a musty smell assailed the traveler's nostrils as he peered into the blackness below. What was that? Something seemed to be moving . . . he put out a hand—and touched a hideous, ice-cold, jelly-like *Thing!* With the shriek of a soul tormented he ran out of the room, down the stairs and out into the night with the vile, nightmarish *Thing* pursuing him.

He ran and ran until he reached a lake where, luckily, he found a rowboat: surely that ghastly creature would not be able to follow him across water? But it could, and it did! The traveler rowed and rowed until he thought his heart would crack, the fearful blob floating in his wake. In the center of the lake he saw an island; gasping, exhausted, he threw himself ashore and curled up in an agony of terror to wait his fate.

The *Thing* emerged from the water and slid toward him until its smelly presence all but engulfed him. He shuddered as a foul tentacle extruded itself from the seething mass, and a ghoulish voice whispered sibilantly, "You're *It*!"

The girl walked into the dark, dark house through the dark, dark hall and down the dark, dark stairs to the dark, dark cellar where there was a dark, dark passageway at the end of which was a dark, dark room. Inside was a dark, dark closet and inside that was an electrician mending the fuse.

Two evil men decided to dig up the grave of a woman who had been buried with a valuable ring on her finger. But try as they might they were unable to pull the ring off the corpse's hand. "We'll have to cut the finger off!" said one of the robbers.

"All right," said the other villain. "I'll do it!"

With the ring in their possession the sinister pair took off. Then a great storm blew up and they began to look around for shelter. In the distance they saw a light, and on approaching saw that it came from a gloomy and strangely forbidding old house. "Let's ask if we can stay the night here," said one of the robbers. So they knocked on the door, and a hideous old woman asked them in. "Would you gentlemen care for some supper?" she asked, cackling weirdly. "Oh, yes please!" they answered, and the old woman took them to the kitchen where she instructed them to sit at a bare wooden table. As she served the food to the hungry pair they noticed that she had a finger missing from her hand! In trembling tones one of the robbers said, "What happened to your finger?"

And the old woman fixed him with a terrible gaze and said, "YOU'VE GOT IT!"

(This story should be told very quietly, and then the last three words yelled out!)

"Sir, what's a gumblestrode?" asked the student innocently.

"How dare you!" roared the angry teacher. "Go to the principal at once!"

In the principal's office the puzzled boy repeated his question. "You awful boy!" yelled the principal. "Get out! And don't come back!"

The unhappy and bewildered boy trudged home. "You're back early," said his father. "What's up?"

"The principal told me to get out," said the boy, "'cause I asked what a gumblestrode was."

"What?" snapped his father. "Get out! Get out of this house! And don't come back!"

In tears the boy wandered the streets until he was spotted by a policemen on his beat. "You're out very late, young man," said the officer. "Can't you go home?" "No," snuffled the miserable youngster. "And all because I asked what a gumblestrode was."

"Did you?" snapped the policeman. "This is a very serious matter. You'd better come with me to the station!" This was too much for the boy; he evaded the policeman's grasp and ran and ran as fast as he could. "Stop that boy!" shouted the officer as he chased in hot pursuit, but as his quarry ran across a main road a truck knocked him down and killed him . . .

A man staying alone one night in a house supposed to be haunted was alarmed to be woken by a mysterious rapping sound. It seemed to be coming from somewhere downstairs, so he got up, put on his bathrobe and cautiously went down to the hall. Still he could hear the rapping noise—was it coming from the cellar? He went down the cellar steps, and the rapping sounded louder and louder. In the cellar was a large cabinet—the rapping was definitely coming from there! Trembling with fear but determined to discover the cause of the sound, the man opened the cabinet door . . . and inside was a large box. Yes, the box was definitely the source of the rapping! Shaking with terror he opened the box—and found a sheet of wrapping paper . . .

An Englishman, an Irishman, and a Scotsman were in jail, and were sentenced to be whipped. "Before I start," said the man with the whip, "I must inform you that by prison rules you are each permitted to have something on your backs to ease the pain." He then said to the Irishman, "What will you have?" "I'll have some Irish whiskey on my back," said the Irishman who had heard that alcohol was good for cuts and bruises. So Irish whiskey was rubbed on the Irishman's back and he was duly whipped. "And what will you have on your back?" the Scotsman was asked; "Scotch whiskey!" he declared stoutly. And Scotch whiskey was rubbed on his back and he was whipped. Then came the Englishman's turn. "And what will you have on your back?" he was asked, to which he replied, "The Irishman!"

An Englishman, an Irishman, and a Scotsman were sentenced to live in a deep pit for ten years, but they were allowed one request each. "I'll have a ten years' supply of Scotch whiskey!" said the Scotsman. "I'll have a ten years' supply of Irish whiskey!" said the Irishman. "I'll have a ten years' supply of cigarettes!" said the Englishman. After ten years they were released: The Scotsman staggered out of the pit and immediately fell dead from alcoholic poisoning. The Irishman also climbed out and fell dead from alcoholic poisoning, but the Englishman climbed out and said, "Anybody got a light?"

"See this ballpoint pen, Brendan? It's the finest in the world. Cost a fortune, but worth every penny. It will write in the hottest deserts, in the Arctic wastes, underwater, in outer space—anywhere and in any environment, it will work exactly the same."

"I've got one like that," replied Brendan not a whit abashed. "Cost me 29¢ at Woolworth's. Works exactly the same wherever you take it."

"For 29¢ How's that?"

"It doesn't work."

A farmer's wife prepared a huge vat of dye in her kitchen garden in order to dye her curtains. Unfortunately one of the lambs wandered into the kitchen garden and fell into the vat. It struggled out a bright pink color, and try as she might the farmer's wife was unable to get the lamb back to its original fleecy white. But as luck would have it a sheep breeder spotted this pink lamb in the field and, deciding it was a new and potentially rare type, offered ten times the normal price to buy it. The farmer's wife shrewdly promised the breeder more pink lambs, and duly dyed as many lambs as were required to make her and her husband's fortune. So that today she is the biggest lamb dyer in the country. . .

An Englishman, an Irishman, and an American were standing at the edge of a fifty-foot cliff. "I'll give $1,000 to whichever of you guys has got the courage to jump over the edge," said the American. Naturally the Englishman and the Irishman refused. "Let's see you do it," they said —and the American immediately leaped off the cliff, landing lightly and unharmed on his toes! So the Englishman jumped off—only to land *splat* on the rocks below; the Irishman jumped off—and he landed *splat* on the rocks. The American then went home and told his wife what had happened. "Oh, that was very bad of you," she declared. "Why didn't you tell them you were Superman!"

Three months before his birthday, little Godfrey was asked by his mother what he would like. "A ping-pong ball, Mom!" he said. A puzzled mother discussed this strange request with Godfrey's father, who also asked the boy what he would like for his birthday. "A ping-pong ball, Dad!" was the answer again. Every few weeks the question was repeated, and the same answer—"A ping-pong ball!"—was always given. Finally Godfrey's birthday arrived, and the small package was handed over. The elated Godfrey rushed up to his bedroom tearing the wrapping paper off his long-awaited present. Mystified, his parents tiptoed up the stairs and peeped in through the door. "Oh," said Godfrey's father, "so *that's* what you wanted a ping-pong ball for . . . !"

An Englishman, an Irishman, and a Scotsman were hiding from bandits up palm trees. The bandit chief called up one tree, "Who's there?" And the Englishman went "Cheep! Cheep!" like a bird. So the bandit chief called up the next tree, "Who's there?" And the Scotsman went "Eeek! Eeek!" like a monkey. So the bandit chief called up the next tree, "Who's there?" And the Irishman went, "Moo-oo!"

An Englishman, an Irishman, and a nun were playing darts. The Englishman threw first and the master of ceremonies called out "One hundred and twenty!" The nun threw next and the master of ceremonies called out "One hundred and sixty!" Then the Irishman threw—but the poor nun had not had a chance to get out of the way, so the master of ceremonies called out, "One nun dead and eighty!"

A biologist spent six months deep in the South American jungle hunting for an extremely rare caterpillar. Finally he found one perfect specimen, which he placed carefully in a special container. The container was placed in a crate, and the crate in a lead box—to make quite sure that the caterpillar reached the London Zoo safely. But when the biologist opened the lead box, the crate and then the special container—no caterpillar was to be seen! Despondent at the thought of six months' work wasted, the biologist decided to make himself a cup of coffee. He turned on the tap for water—and what do you think came out? *(You will of course receive the answer "the caterpillar," to which you reply)* No, water!

A terrible thing happened to me yesterday! I was with my Mom in the supermarket doing some shopping. She asked me to look after her basket while she went to get something from the other end of the store, and while I was waiting the manager came up and said I was trying to shoplift! He took me into his office and said he was going to call the police; I was so scared, and I knew my Mom would be wondering where I had got to, so I leaned out of the window to see if I could see her. Well, the manager thought I was trying to escape, so he pulled my leg... just as I'm pulling yours now!

A traveler stuck miles from anywhere in the country was relieved to find a small hotel; the bad news was that it looked extremely uninviting and sinister. However, the traveler didn't want to spend the night in his car, and so he asked for a room. All seemed quite normal, if somewhat quiet, and the only thing he found disturbing was a large red button by the door of his room. What was it for? There was no notice to explaining it, so what could it be? An alarm bell? A service bell? All night long he lay, tossing and turning, worrying about the purpose of the mysterious button. By morning he was absolutely exhausted, not having slept a wink. He packed his bag wearily, but just as he was leaving to go downstairs for breakfast, his curiosity got the better of him. Plucking up his courage he jabbed firmly at the red button—and the ceiling light came on...

Three knights were arguing over which of them was the bravest. "I fought a dragon in the air," said the first, "and cut its head off!" "I fought a dragon under the sea," said the second, "and cut its tail off!" "I cut the tail off a snail," said the third. "That's not very brave!" scoffed the other two. "Well," came the reply, "it was a dragon (dragging) on the ground!"

An Englishman, an Irishman, and a Scotsman had gone mountaineering. An avalanche had cut off the way forward and the way back, leaving them stuck on the very edge of a steep drop of two thousand yards. While they were debating between themselves what was to be done a fairy appeared. "I can see your predicament," said the fairy, "and I will help you if I can. You may have one wish each, but my powers are limited and I can only change you into birds."

"Very well," said the Englishman, "I'll be an eagle." The fairy waved her magic wand, and immediately the Englishman was changed into a noble eagle; he stepped off the edge of the cliff and soared away to safety.

"I'll be a hawk," said the Scotsman—again the fairy waved her wand and the Scotsman, now a beautiful hawk, soared away to safety.

"What bird would you like to be?" said the fairy to the Irishman. "Er, a penguin" said the Irishman . . .

Another Englishman, another Irishman, and another Scotsman were also trapped on a cliff edge, when again the Good Fairy appeared. "I can help you out of your predicament, gentlemen," she declared. "I can grant you one wish each—you can choose wherever you would like to be."

The Englishman immediately stepped forward. "England," he said—and straightaway the Good Fairy sent him back to England.

The Scotsman stepped forward. "Scotland!" he declared—and straightaway he found himself back in Scotland.

The Irishman stepped forward and stumbled over a rock, "Oh hell . . . !" he muttered—and straightaway. . . .

Help Wanted
or Mind Your Own Business

"My brother's got a good job."
  "What's that?"
  "Test pilot for Kleenex."

Who earns a living by driving customers away?
  A cabbie.

"I'm the boss and you're nothing! What are you?"
  "Nothing."
  "And what am I?"
  "Boss over nothing."
  "Bah! You're next to an idiot."
  "Very well. I'll move."

"My grandfather was a ship's carpenter. He was a champion poopdeck maker. He made five hundred poopdecks and then he died."

"Why?"

"He was all pooped out."

"Are you still working at that florist's?"

"No, I got fired."

"Why?"

"I had to put the cards into the floral tributes and I got two of them mixed up. The flowers going to a wedding I thought were going to a funeral, so I put in a card which read "With Deepest Sympathy" . . . and the flowers going to the funeral had a wedding card in them."

"What did it say?"

"Hope You'll Be Happy In Your New Home!"

At a business conference a self-made millionaire approached the president of a rival company and said, "I started my business life working for you."

"Really?" said the president. "I'm afraid I don't recall . . ."

"Yes, indeed," said the millionaire smugly. "Thirty years ago I started as an office boy for your company. Do you remember giving me a message to deliver to the mailroom?"

"Oh, yes," said the president. "Now I remember. Any answer?"

"Boss, there's a man here to see you."

"Tell him to take a chair."

"Why, is he buying old furniture?"

"Is it difficult to be a coroner?"

"Oh, yes. You have to take a stiff exam."

"Why do you want to be an astronomer?"

"I think it's a heavenly job!"

"I want a haircut, please."

"Certainly, sir. Which one?"

"How's the trampoline business?"

"Oh, up and down."

"Did you hear about old Harry? He's become a big time operator."

"Really? What does he do?"

"Winds up Big Ben."

"This bread is nice and warm!"
    "It should be—the cat's been sitting on it all day!"

"Mr. Butcher, have you got a sheep's head?"
    "No, ma'am, it's just the way I part my hair."

"Two pounds of dog's food, please."
    "Certainly, sir. Shall I wrap it or will you eat it here?"

What job has plenty of openings?
    A doorman.

Why did the lazy man get a job in a bakery?
    'Cause he wanted a good loaf.

"Late again, Slattery? Why don't you get an alarm clock?"
    "I did, sir, but it keeps going off while I'm asleep!"

"I say, waiter! Why is there a yellow line around my table?"

"Oh, you'd better move, sir. There's no parking there."

"I say, waiter! There are five flies in my soup!"

"Gosh, sir! Just one more and you'd have a world record!"

Did you hear about the worker in a banana-packing firm?

He got fired for throwing the bent ones away...

A boy went into a pet shop and said to the man behind the counter, "Have you got any parrot seed?"

"Oh, you've got a parrot, have you?" said the man.

"No," said the boy, "but I'd like to grow one!"

"What would you like?" asked the waiter in the seafood restaurant.

"Shark and fries," replied the customer. "And make it snappy!"

A diner in a restaurant was handed the menu by the waiter who, the diner was upset to notice, stood by the table scratching his bottom. "Say, waiter," said the customer icily, "have you got an itchy bottom?"

"No, sir," replied the waiter. "Only what's on the menu!"

"Say, waiter! There's a fly in my soup!"

"Well, throw him a doughnut—he'll need a lifesaver."

A worker on a building site rushed up to the foreman. "Boss! Boss!" he cried. "Someone just dropped a trowel from the top of the scaffolding and sliced my ear off!" Immediately the foreman organized a search party to find the ear in the hope that surgeons might be able to sew it on again. "Here it is!" cried one of the searchers, waving an ear. "No, that's not it," said the injured workman. "Mine had a pencil behind it!"

This'll Kill You!
or Dying of Laughter

What is the best way for a ghostbuster to keep fit?
  He must exorcise regularly.

What do you call twin ghosts who keep ringing doorbells?
  Dead ringers.

What is the ghost's favorite kind of tune?
  A haunting melody.

Who speaks at the ghosts' press conference?
  A spooksman.

Who said "Shiver me timbers!" on the ghost ship?
  The skeleton crew.

Why are a monster's fingers never more than eleven inches long?
  'Cause if they were twelve inches they'd be a foot.

Why is a turkey like an evil little creature?
  'Cause it's always a-gobblin'. . .

Where did Dracula keep his money?
  In a blood bank.

How does a witch tell the time?
  With a witch watch.

Why was Frankenstein never lonely?
  He was good at making friends.

Why did the skeleton go to the party?
    For a rattling good time!

Why are ghosts bad at telling lies?
    'Cause you can always see through them.

Why are vampires mad?
    'Cause they're bats.

What did the man say when he met the three-headed mon-ster?
    "Hello, Hello, Hello!"

What is a gargoyle?
    Something you take for a sore throat.

Where do you find giant snails?
    On the end of giants' fingers.

Why wouldn't the skeleton jump off the cliff?
    'Cause it didn't have any guts.

What is Dracula's favorite pudding?
    Leeches and scream.

The Ghost teacher was showing the little Ghosts how to walk through walls. "Now did you all follow that, Ghosties?" she asked. "If not, I'll just go through it again . . ."

Why does Dracula live in a coffin?
    'Cause the rent is low.

What did one ghost say to the other ghost?
    "Do you believe in people?"

What does a monster eat after a tooth extraction?
    The dentist.

What trees do monsters like best?
    Cemetrees.

If you were surrounded by Dracula, Frankenstein's monster, a ghost, and a werewolf, what would you be hoping?
   That you were at a costume party.

Why are monsters forgetful?
   'Cause everything you tell them goes in one ear and out the others.

What is the best way to speak to a monster?
   From far away.

Where do monsters study?
   At ghoullege.

What do you call a friendly and handsome monster?
   A failure.

What has webbed feet and fangs?
   Count Quackula.

Why did Frankenstein's monster give up boxing?
  'Cause he didn't want to spoil his looks.

Why is Baron Frankenstein fun at parties?
  'Cause he'll have you in stitches.

What do vampires cross the sea in?
  Blood vessels.

What is the best thing to do if a monster breaks down your front door?
  Run out through the back door.

What do monsters put on their roast beef?
  Grave-y.

What is a ghost's favorite drink?
  Demonade.

What kind of ices do monsters prefer?
  I-screams for help.

Did you hear about the stupid ghost?
  He climbed over walls.

Where do monsters travel?
  From ghost to ghost.

Why is Dracula so unpopular?
  'Cause he's a pain in the neck.

What did the vampire say to the dentist after he'd had all his teeth out?
  "Fangs for the memory!"

Can a toothless vampire still bite you?
  No, but he can give you a nasty suck!

What do ghosts like to play at parties?
  Haunt and seek.

"Don't eat with your fingers, dear," said the Mommy ghost to the little ghost. "Use the shovel!"

Why did the baby monster push his father in the freezer?
   'Cause he wanted frozen pop.

Travelers' Tales

PILOT: "Mayday! Mayday! Starboard engine on fire!"
GROUND CONTROL: "State your height and position."
PILOT: "I'm five foot eight and I'm sitting in the cockpit."

"Last time my wife and I traveled on the ferry from England to France we had six meals."

"Six meals for that short crossing?"

"Three down and three up."

The young midshipman was being examined on his seamanship. "Now, then, Scuttle," said the examiner, "you are about to enter the harbor when a severe storm blows up. What do you do?"

"I don't try to enter the harbor, sir. I let go of an anchor and ride out the storm."

"Very good. But supposing the storm abates, you try and haul up the anchor and the chain snaps—and another storm blows up. What do you do?"

"I'd throw out the spare anchor, sir."

"Excellent. Now, the second storm abates; you try and raise the spare anchor, and again the chain snaps just as a third storm blows up. What do you do?"

"I'd throw out a third anchor, sir."

"Just a minute. Where are you getting all these anchors from?"

"The same place you're getting the storms."

"When we got to Miami the hotel was so full I had to sleep on a door across two sawhorses."

"Was it comfortable?"

"Oh, yes. But a bit drafty round the letter slot."

A driver who had the misfortune to run over a woman's dog was extremely apologetic. "I really am very sorry, ma'am," he said. "I will of course replace your dog."

"If you like," she replied, "but are you any good at catching rats?"

An extremely rich businessman found himself in a small New England hotel where his wealth and importance seemed to be quite unknown, and to his chagrin he was treated with no more and no less respect than any other guest. Determined to show his worth, at breakfast he said loudly to the waiter, "Bring me $10 worth of bacon and eggs!" Not a bit abashed, the waiter said, "Sorry, sir, but we don't serve children's portions!"

A French hitchhiker in England was delighted when a motorist stopped at his thumbing signal. "Want a lift?" asked the motorist.

"Oui, oui," agreed the Frenchman.

"Not in my car you don't!"

An American visitor to England was wandering around a small county town, and got into conversation with a local. "What do you do for entertainment around here?" he asked. "Is there a movie house?"

"No, no movie house," said the local.

"A theatre?"

"No, no theatre."

"A disco?"

"No, no disco."

"So what is there in this town?"

"Well, we lads like to go to the grocers' shop and watch the bacon slicer."

"That's fun, is it?"

"Well, she's a lovely girl."

A motorist driving through the country stopped for a hitchhiker who was holding the halter of a cow. "I can give you a lift," he said, "but I can't take your cow."

"Don't worry," said the hitchhiker, "she'll follow us in her own time."

So the hitchhiker got in and the motorist started up. He drove at thirty miles an hour and the cow lolloped along behind him; he drove at forty miles an hour and the cow was still lolloping along behind; he drove at fifty miles an hour yet the cow was somehow managing to keep pace with him. But he noticed in his mirror that the cow seemed to be tiring as her tongue was hanging out of her mouth. "I'm worried about your cow," said the motorist to his passenger, "her tongue is hanging out of her mouth to the right."

"Oh, that's all right," said the hitchhiker, "that means she wants to pass you . . . !"

A man in the United States decided to make some money by getting himself run over. He stood at a bus stop and stuck his leg out so that when the bus arrived it ran him over. He was in the hospital for three months and received $50,000 in compensation. Then he went to France and tried the same trick, this time receiving 200,000 francs in compensation. But when he came to Britain and stood at a bus stop with his leg sticking out he died of pneumonia . . .

A man and his friend were driving through the center of town, and the driver's handling of the car was very erratic. "Tell me, Joey," said his increasingly perturbed friend, "why do you shut your eyes every time we come to a red light?"

"Why not?" retorted Joey. "When you've seen one you've seen 'em all . . . !"

A traveler stranded in the desert asked a passerby for water. "Sorry," said the passerby, "I have no water. Only ties which I am taking to market." The traveler staggered on through the burning sands and met another passerby. "Water," he gasped. "Please, give me water!"

"I have no water," said the second passerby. "Only these ties, which I am taking to market." Nearly dead from thirst the traveler met a third passerby—but he was also only taking ties to market. And so the wretched traveler lurched on, half-dead from thirst, until to his joy he saw a hotel! He crawled into the lobby on his hands and knees and croaked out, "Water! For the love of Allah, give me water!"

"Sorry, sir," said the desk clerk. "We don't allow anyone in without a tie!"

Having asked for shelter for the night at a monastery in England the traveler was surprised and delighted at being given a magnificent supper of succulent fish and chips. "That was absolutely superb!" he enthused to the monk who had been serving him. "That piece of fish was wonderful, and beautifully cooked. And as for the chips—

they were the tastiest chips I've ever had in my life. Well done, Brother." "Oh, you must thank Brother Ambrose for those," came the reply. "I'm the fish friar—he's the chip monk . . ."

A man sat on a train chewing gum and staring vacantly into space, when suddenly an old lady sitting opposite said, "It's no good you talking to me, young man, I'm completely deaf!"

Fifty Irishmen were traveling on a train. "Sure and it's too crowded in this compartment," said the leader. "The next one's empty—Let's use that one." So at the next stop the fifty Irishmen got off—and all promptly went into the empty compartment!

"You deliberately drove into my car!" said the first driver to the second. "Why did you do it?"

"I saw that sticker in your back window," came the reply. "It says 'Give Blood' so I thought I'd give you some of mine!"

As the double-decker bus arrived at the stop, a man at the head of the line took out his eye, bounced it hard on the pavement, caught it, put it back in his eye, and boarded the bus.

"What did you do that for?" asked the amazed conductor.

"I just wanted to see," replied the man, "if there was any room on top!"

"I got a puncture in the back tire of my bike yesterday."

"Bad luck. Did you mend it?"

"No, I just raised the seat."

Just as the jet was about to take off, a nervous old lady called for a stewardess. "I've never been in an airplane before," she said. "Tell me, my dear, what happens if we run out of fuel?"

"Don't worry, madam," replied the young woman. "We all get out and push!"

Whenever there is a car accident each driver involved has to write a report of the occurrence for the insurance company. The following are actual quotations from some of these reports:

"Coming home, I drove into the wrong house and collided with a tree I didn't have."

"I thought my window was down, but I found it was up when I put my hand through it."

"I collided with a stationary truck coming the other way."

"A van backed through my windshield into my wife's face."

"A pedestrian hit me and went under my car."

"He was all over the road, and I had to swerve a number of times before I hit him."

"In an attempt to kill a fly I drove into a telephone pole."

"I had been driving my car for forty years when I fell asleep at the wheel."

"My car was legally parked as it backed into the other vehicle."

"An invisible car came out of nowhere, struck my vehicle and vanished."

"I told the police that I was not injured, but on removing my hat I found that I had a fractured skull."

"The pedestrian had no idea which direction to go, so I ran over him."

"I saw the slow-moving, sad-faced old gentleman as he bounced off the hood of my car."

"The indirect cause of this accident was the little man in a small car with a mustache."

"I was thrown from my car as it left the road. I was later found in a ditch by some cows "

"The telephone pole was approaching fast and I was attempting to swerve out of its path when it struck my front."

"I was on my way to the doctor when my rear end gave way, causing me to have an accident."

"I pulled away from the side of the road, glanced at my mother-in-law and drove into the river."

An intrepid explorer in the days of the old Wild West was captured by an Indian tribe notorious for their habit of skinning their victims alive. "Before you die," said the chief solemnly, "you are allowed one wish. What will it be, white man?"

"A fork, if you please," said the explorer. Bemused, the chief ordered a fork to be given to the white man, who immediately began plunging it into himself all over, saying, "I'll make sure you don't make a canoe out of me!"

THEY'RE MORE THAN

FUNNY...

THEY'RE LAUGH-OUT-LOUD

HYSTERICAL!